Business

Personal Effectiveness & Career Development

Hodder & Stoughton

A MEMBER OF THE HODDER HEADLINE GROUP

Orders; please contact Bookpoint Ltd, 78 Milton Park, Abingdon, Oxon OX14 4TD. Telephone: (44) 01235 400414, Fax: (44) 01235 400454. Lines are open from 9.00–6.00, Monday to Saturday, with a 24 hour message answering service. Email address: orders@bookpoint.co.uk

British Library Cataloguing in Publication Data
A catalogue record for this title is available from the British Library

ISBN 0 340 74294 1

First published 1999
Impression number   10 9 8 7 6 5 4 3 2 1
Year   2005 2004 2003 2002 2001 2000 1999

Typeset by GreenGate Publishing Services, Tonbridge, Kent.
Printed in Great Britain for Hodder and Stoughton Educational, a division of Hodder Headline Plc, 338 Euston Road, London NW1 3BH, by Redwood Books, Trowbridge, Wiltshire

Contents

68624

the Institute of Management

F O U N D A T I O N

The mission of the Institute of Management (IM) is to promote the art and science of management.

The Institue embraces all levels of management from student to chief executive and supports its own Foundation which provides a unique portfolio of services for all managers, enabling them to develop skills and achieve management excellence.

For information on the various levels and benefits of membership, please contact:

Department HS
Institute of Management
Cottingham Road
Corby
Northants NN17 1TT
Tel: 01536 204222
Fax: 01536 201651

Preface

The first Business Checklists were launched by the Institute of Management in 1995. They met with immediate success from managers in all sectors of commerce and industry, and in organisations of all shapes and sizes.

They originated from one simple idea – that managers did not have the time, or indeed the inclination, to plough through heavy tomes of turgid prose in order to unearth the odd nugget or two which might enable them to do their jobs a little better. They also drew their origins from a former series of Checklists by the British Institute of Management which had been successful in the 1970s.

So why are they so successful? Basically because they cut out unnecessary waffle. They express in clear, concise language what managers need to know, and are presented in a consistent format so that it is easy to pick out the bits you want. They have a wide application, outside business as well as inside, and in small or large organisations: introducing a concept or technique, explaining the pros and cons, dos and don'ts, and steps to follow to get you started. They also provide further pointers for those who do have the time, inclination or need to pursue the topic in greater depth.

Updated and revised since their launch, the Business Checklists are here presented for the first time in a series of books which bring them together under broad management functions.

How are the subjects chosen? Not by guesswork or experts who think they know best, but by demand. The Institute's Management Information Centre handles over 50,000 enquiries a year so the Centre's researchers not only have a good idea of what managers are looking for but also how they want it delivered.

Each checklist follows a similar pattern:

MCI Standards

The MCI Management Standards are the underpinning structure for many vocational management qualifications. Each checklist identifies the appropriate subject content of the standards that it meets.

Definition

Clarifies the coverage of the checklist, highlighting both what is and what is not included in its scope.

Advantages and disadvantages

Each checklist highlights the benefits and pitfalls of the topic, providing a quick insight into the experiences of others.

Action checklist

The core of the checklist is the step-by-step sequence, written in jargon-free language and designed to help readers get to grips with a task quickly.

Dos and don'ts

A brief summary of the key items to remember – and to avoid – on each topic.

Useful reading and organisations

Sources of additional information for readers wishing to investigate the topic further.

Thought starters

Some introductory ideas to help readers begin to approach the subject in a practical way.

Although the Business Checklists constitute a wide-ranging, but concise, library of management know-how, we don't pretend – yet – that they are complete. As they are being continually updated and revised, please get in touch with the Institute of Management's Information Centre in Corby if you have suggestions for future editions.

Bob Norton
Head of Information Services
Institute of Management.

Writing your CV

> **This checklist is designed to help those compiling or updating a Curriculum Vitae.**

MCI Standards

This checklist has relevance for the MCI Management Standards: Key Role C – Manage People.

Definition

A Curriculum Vitae is a vital tool for job hunting. Essentially it is a document which describes you – your career, education, and personal details – painting an attractive but accurate portrait of your abilities, achievements and interests.

Action checklist

1. Aim to produce a CV which has impact, is factual and brief

Your CV should be:

- positive – more than just giving a list of responsibilities
- clear – written in understandable language
- neat – the best standard you can achieve in content and layout.
- short – preferably two sides of A4. It should never exceed three pages.

It is essential that your CV is as easy to read as possible. Use both headings (Personal, Education, Experience etc) and bullet points.

2. Identifying detail

This important information forms the head of the document and consists of:

- full name
- address
- telephone numbers: home and others where you are contactable.

Very often, organisations remove this information to meet their equal opportunities policies.

3. Decide on a suitable format for your CV

The two most used CV formats are chronological or functional in style.

- Chronological – as it suggests, this CV follows your career back in an historical manner and works well for those who have significant incremental moves. However, gaps on the CV are very obvious.

- Functional – this style of CV highlights the main skill areas such as management, people, operations, finance, budgets and IT. It is particularly appropriate for those who have developed their career on the basis of their transferable skills.

Of the two, the chronological CV is still the most widely used.

4. Carry out your preparation

Consider your career, and starting with your last role work backwards in chronological order stating:

- job title – with clarification if necessary
- outline of responsibilities – including the number of people managed
- main achievements – the areas where you have made positive contributions.

The most detailed information should be provided about your most recent post, with detail reducing as you go back in time (unless a post was of special relevance to the one you are applying for). Posts held more than about 10 years ago should usually only be listed by responsibilities.

5. Describe your achievements as your own

A CV is essentially a selling tool. By using active words, such as analysed, achieved, created, developed, designed, implemented, specialised or led, a positive picture of your skills can be developed. Use phrases such as:

- 'The systems I designed are now contributing to the success of the organisation.'
- 'I designed and successfully introduced new procedures.'

This approach is valuable for either chronological or functional formats.

6. Note your educational experiences, including short courses

Again, in chronological order list:

- schools/colleges attended at secondary level and above
- qualifications obtained
- professional qualifications and memberships.

If at all possible, each qualification should be limited to just one line. If you are a regular attendee of short courses, include only those of relevance to the post applied for.

Think carefully about where education should be placed in your CV. If you have been studying in the last five years, or if you have completed a qualification relevant to the role, place education towards the beginning.

7. Decide on the further personal detail you wish to include

This information may include:

- date of birth
- marital status and gender
- driving licence
- hobbies – but try to strike a balance between the picture of someone whose leisure activities are so numerous and absorbing that they leave no time for work, and someone with no outside interests
- career aspirations – but only include these if they 'fit' with the job for which you are applying.

8. Consider who will see your CV

The preliminary sift of applications is frequently carried out by a comparatively junior employee who will in general spend about a minute scanning each CV. At this stage they are looking for a reason to reject candidates. Therefore:

- check and double-check your spelling
- get someone else to read your draft through
- ensure the presentation is clear and easy to read
- CVs must ALWAYS be typed or word processed.

Some companies scan CVs onto a computer and then search for specific key words. It is therefore sensible to try to mention the current buzz-words in your area.

9. Write a covering letter

Covering letters are also important. You should use them to tailor your experience to the opportunity or organisation and to summarise key elements of your CV. Below are some useful phrases.

Applying in response to an advertisement

'I am writing in response to the above advertisement and wish to apply for the position outlined.' '...As requested, I enclose a copy of my CV for your consideration. I am seeking an appointment where my experience can be fully utilised and I would be pleased to discuss this post in more detail.'

One successful style of letter writing lists the requirements outlined in the advertisement with your skills and experience – this clearly displays how you match the role.

Speculative applications

'I intend to progress my career with the accent on...I would welcome a meeting with you to discuss my CV in greater depth in the context of any suitable vacancies in your organisation.' 'A copy of my CV is enclosed. If you feel my experience could be usefully applied within..., I would be pleased to meet with you to discuss existing or potential openings.'

Dos and don'ts for CV writing

Do

- Be simple in your message.
- Ensure that the layout is easy to follow.
- Create plenty of white space.
- Sell yourself and use your achievements.
- Use current key or buzz words.
- Choose a format which works best for you.
- Pilot your CV with colleagues and friends.
- Put yourself in the shoes of the reader.

Don't

- Lie.
- Assume your name will get you noticed.
- Be afraid to get advice.
- Lose your individualism.

Useful reading

Successful CVs in a week, 2nd ed, Steve Morris, London: Hodder & Stoughton, 1998
The perfect CV: how to get the job you really want, Rev ed, Tom Jackson and Ellen Jackson, London: Piaktus, 1997
CVs and written applications, 2nd ed, Judy Skeats, London: Ward Lock, 1994
The perfect CV: all you need to get it right first time, 2nd ed, Max Eggert, London: Century, 1992

Thought starters

- You have 8 seconds to make an impression with your CV. What impression does yours create in 8 seconds? Ask a reader.
- CVs should be about the future. Is it clear what contribution you could make to an organisation and what your future career objective is?
- CVs are also about the past: does yours summarise adequately your past to your satisfaction?
- When was the last time you updated your CV?

The Formal Interview: Effective Face to Face Communications

This checklist is designed to enable you to communicate more effectively face to face.

MCI Standards

This checklist has relevance for the MCI Management Standards: Key Roles C and D – Manage People and Manage Information.

Definition

Within the organisation, communications can be upwards, with your own boss or other senior staff; downwards, with junior staff who work for you or for other managers; or sideways, with colleagues. Externally, face to face communications cover a range of encounters, from those with suppliers or clients to those with colleagues from similar organisations or competitors.

Action checklist

1. Clarify the purpose of the communication and its expected outcome

Work out what you expect to achieve from the encounter. Distinguish between your long term goal (for example to ensure that a major project is delivered on time and within budget) and what you expect to achieve from the particular meeting. This will provide a benchmark against which to judge whether the communication was effective. It will also provide a marker for when you should end the meeting.

2. Work out which aspects of the encounter you can, and should, plan in advance

Decide how much of the communication you can plan in advance. Do this where the outcome is known and critical, and needs to be unambiguous.

This includes key contract meetings with clients or suppliers, disciplinary interviews with junior staff or critical progress meetings with senior staff. Only take an unstructured approach where the purpose of the communication is to seek information or to counsel.

3. Plan your use of space

Create and maintain a distance between you and the other person that is conducive to relaxed communication – too close and you will be intimidating; too far away and you will be threatening. If you need to compete, negotiate or argue, take up a position opposite the other person. If you need cooperation, sit side by side. For counselling or eliciting information, a neutral position at 90 degrees to the other person is best. Be wary of using your desk as an artificial barrier to reinforce your status.

4. Set a time limit

Be realistic and set a time limit within which you can reasonably expect to achieve your planned outcome. With open-ended communications, such as counselling interviews, discuss the timing with the interviewee first. Don't arbitrarily end a communication.

5. Ensure you are in the right role to achieve the outcome you want

Assume the role you need to secure your outcome, such as tutor, adviser, boss or salesperson. Do this consciously and don't slip into another role during the meeting or allow yourself to be led into one. Ensure you select the role that is appropriate: don't attempt to discipline someone if you have assumed the role of friendly adviser. Only change roles if the outcome you are seeking changes during the communication.

6. Create rapport before you begin

Smile: don't launch into your pitch immediately. Find out how the respondent is feeling and ask friendly questions to encourage the flow of information before setting out your own case. Assume junior staff will be inhibited even if they appear at ease: try to establish that you are a pleasant person to do business with.

7. Adopt the right tone

Use a tone that is appropriate to the role you need to play without appearing artificial. If you are seeking information, be relaxed, open and warm; if you are conducting a disciplinary interview be firm and business-like. Be wary of using the wrong tone or style or you will send a confused message to the listener.

8. Set the right scene

Begin by quickly providing background to the encounter and summarising previous meetings or conversations. Ask for an update or new information and avoid second-guessing what the other person will say. Present your own case openly and don't be devious or clever. Aim to concentrate both sides' minds on the intellectual issues before progressing to remedial action and a solution to the problem.

9. Understand how the values, attitudes and expectations of the other person will affect the outcome

Be aware of the other person's reference point. How do they view the issue and what barriers will this throw up to you achieving the outcome? Understand their values but be wary of introducing prejudice and assuming that all employees in a certain category will view an issue the same way.

10. Understand and manage the pressures brought to the interview by both sides

Be aware of the possible concerns the other person might bring to the encounter which could block progress: about their competence to do a job, their own career prospects, what colleagues might think, or whether they might be asked to rush a job and compromise on quality. Recognise and face up to the pressures on you: the need to be acting fairly, legal requirements, deadlines and time pressures.

11. Use the right skills to achieve the outcome you want

Strike the right balance between asking open questions at the beginning to elicit information and specific questions to tie down details. Be alive to the other person's non-verbal signals and use them to check that your questions are being understood and correctly interpreted. Use signals and gestures yourself to reinforce your message and convey shades of attitude and expression.

12. Manage the interview towards an outcome

Actively steer the encounter toward a conclusion. Use closed questions to check your understanding and assumptions. Identify the main points the other person has made and use their words to summarise the key conclusions.

13. Once you've achieved your original objective, stop!

If you have set a clear objective for the meeting and you have achieved it, stop. Don't dilute the impact of what you have said by straying on to another agenda or reviewing the content of the meeting. Being tightly focused on the outcome of a communication will gain you time and effectiveness.

Dos and don'ts for the formal interview

Do

- Get your timing right and adjust to the other person's rhythms of speech – otherwise you risk appearing either hesitant or overly brusque.
- Be aware of the impact of your own body language, posture, gestures and non-verbal signals – only a small portion of understanding comes from words.
- Put yourself in the position of the other person before you begin speaking – imagine what effect your words will have and what barriers exist to their being understood.

Don't

- Set an over-ambitious agenda for a face to face meeting – you will confuse the other person and finish without achieving any of your objectives.
- Adopt the wrong role or style for an encounter or allow yourself to be led into one that is inappropriate.

Useful reading

Contemporary business communication, Louis E Boone and David L Kurtz, Englewood Cliffs, NJ: Prentice Hall, 1994

Management face to face, Derek Torrington, New York: Prentice Hall, 1991

Putting it across, Angela Heylin, London: Michael Joseph, 1991

The communicating manager: a guide to working effectively with people, Mike Dutfield and Chris Eling, Shaftesbury: Element Books, 1990

Thought starters

- What role do other people normally expect you to play in face to face encounters – is it always the right one to achieve the outcome you want?
- Which communications are you least comfortable with? Which skills do you need to develop to reinforce your confidence in handling them?

How to Succeed at Interviews

This checklist is for those who want to improve their performance, and ultimately their success, at selection interviews.

MCI Standards

This checklist has relevance for the MCI Management Standards: Key Role C – Manage People.

Definition

Interviews are formal face to face meetings between existing or potential employers and existing or potential employees. This checklist concentrates on selection interviews: those interviews which assess (or partly assess) an individual's suitability for a job either inside or outside their current organisation.

Action checklist

1. Clarify your objectives

Always clarify what you want from the interview – a job offer, more information on the job and the organisation, an opportunity to meet the decision makers. If your objective is unclear it will be difficult to hide this from the interviewers – and these people could be significant in your future.

2. Do your research

To succeed at interview, first undertake some research to find out as much as you can about the interview, the job and the organisation.

The Interview:
- how to get there
- who will interview you
- the format of the interview (*group, one to one, tests, presentations*).

The Job:

- extent of duties and reporting relationships
- history
- expectations
- conditions of employment and location of work.

The Organisation:

- history, ownership and products
- size, structure and location of sites
- stability, prosperity and financial strength
- reputation, strengths and weaknesses
- competitors.

3. Know yourself

To succeed at interview, you must make an impression that will bring attention to you as THE CANDIDATE for the job rather than just another runner. Understand what makes you special, what makes you fit the position, and what you can offer. Satisfy yourself that you know how to convey these messages to the interviewer.

4. Prepare yourself for success

Positive thinking is an important part of your preparation. Compare the thoughts: 'I'm just here to make up the numbers' with 'I've been chosen from a large number of other candidates'. Try to relax mentally and physically beforehand.

5. Your appearance

First impressions count. You make an impression before you respond to any questions. Ensure that your appearance is smart:

- appropriate clothes are essential
- finer points including hair, nails and shoes, must not be forgotten
- avoid too much scent or after-shave
- avoid extremes of colour or pattern in clothes.

6. Prepare for questioning

Think about the questions you are likely to be asked, and prepare your thoughts on possible answers. Questions may include:

- **Self-assessment:** What can you do for us that someone else can't? Why should we appoint you? What are your strengths and what limits you? How would you describe your own personality? How do you react to pressure and deal with deadlines?

- **Work history and experience:** Tell me a little about yourself. Why are you leaving your present position? What have been your successes?

- **Organisation:** How much do you know about our organisation? How long would it take you to make a meaningful contribution to our organisation? What important trends do you see in our industry?

- **Job:** Why do you want to work for us? What do you find most attractive about this position? What seems least attractive to you? What do you look for in a job?

- **Management style:** What is your management style? Are you a good manager? What do you think is the most difficult thing about being a manager? If I spoke to your former boss, what would s/he say were your strengths and weaknesses?

- **General interests and knowledge:** What was the last book you read, film you saw, sporting event you attended? What do you do to relax?

7. At the interview

Before the interview begins, there are certain steps to take which will help you succeed.

- Ensure you arrive at your interview with sufficient time to enable you to relax a little beforehand.
- When meeting the interviewer(s) smile, and use good eye contact.
- Use good body language (sit upright and lean slightly forward) to convey an impression of interested alertness.
- Don't fidget with your hands or keep crossing and uncrossing your legs etc.

8. Answering questions

Questions asked during interviews are designed to help the interviewer learn more about you and whether you would be suited to the job. Listen attentively to questions and answer them succinctly. Remember you are interviewing the employer at the same time as they are interviewing you.

When replying to questions you should:

- keep to the point
- structure your answer so that it is logical and easily understood
- maintain good, but not obsessive, eye contact
- speak out with confidence and ensure you can be heard clearly
- look prepared and have appropriate information to hand
- project interest in the organisation and job, and be interesting in your replies and questions
- be honest: admit to limitations, don't exaggerate accomplishments.

Answer the questions in a way which demonstrates your qualities. Use statements which:

- are assertive
- begin 'I am ...'
- show that you are proud of your achievements.

9. Prepare your own questions

You may be asked if you have any questions at the end of the interview – prepare some in advance, relating them to the job or organisation. This helps demonstrate your interest. Don't relate them all to money or conditions of employment.

10. Deal positively with the closing moments of the interview

Last impressions are important too. Thank the interviewers for their time, re-affirm your interest in the position and state that you look forward to hearing from them in the near future – even if you have already decided you don't want the job.

Dos and don'ts for successful interviews

Do
- Arrive in good time.
- Take time in answering questions and give concise answers.
- Speak up and speak clearly.
- Present information that will help your case.
- Be willing to affirm your viewpoint in an assertive way.
- Ask your own questions.
- Be relaxed and think positively.
- End on a confident, optimistic note and deal with the closing moments well.

Don't
- Interrupt, argue, overreact or get on your soap box.
- Be evasive, speak too quickly or give long, involved answers.
- Criticise third parties, or former employers.
- Become too familiar.
- Be tense.

Useful reading
Succeeding at interviews in a week, 2nd ed, Mo Shapiro and Alison Straw, London: Hodder & Stoughton, 1999

The perfect interview: how to get the job you really want, 2nd ed, John D Drake, New York: Amacom, 1996

Succeed at your job interview, George Heaviside, London: BBC Books, 1993

The perfect interview: all you need to get it right first time, Max Eggert, London: Century Books, 1992

Great answers to tough interview questions: how to get the job you want, Martyn Yate, London: Kogan Page, 1986

Useful addresses

If there are areas that you suspect, or are told, consistently let you down – seek help or a second opinion. Investigate sources of help such as:

● colleges/adult education centres
● TEC's/LEC's
● careers counsellors or local careers services
● professional institutes

Thought starters

● You don't have the time to experiment with being interviewed – only poor performers get lots of interview practice.
● Don't be afraid to ask! Information helps to relieve the anxiety and trepidation we all feel approaching the unknown.

The Woman Returner – Getting Back to Work

This checklist is for those women preparing to re-enter employment. Many women leave paid employment due to family responsibilities, but once these have changed or been resolved, they find that their confidence to return to work has been eroded or their skills are now out of date. This checklist forms a step-by-step guide to help address these problems.

MCI Standards

This checklist has relevance for the MCI Management Standards: Key Role C – Manage People.

Definition

Woman returner is a broad term used to describe any woman returning to paid employment, whether full or part-time, after a substantial period away from work, usually taken to care for children or elderly relatives.

Returners are the norm amongst the female workforce: the full-time life-long career woman with a family is still the exception.

Action checklist

1. List your skills

If you are returning to work after a long absence, be imaginative in identifying skills you have already acquired: define the tasks you perform on a daily basis and the skills used. Running a home demands good time, project and financial management skills and the ability to organise and negotiate. Many people in work will not have this breadth of experience. Take into account any voluntary or unpaid work, for example with schools or local committees.

2. Translate your skills into areas of strength

Classify the skills you have identified into different groups, for example, people management or financial planning. This can be used to demonstrate your strengths to potential employers. Consider which skills you most enjoy applying: this will give you pointers to possible areas of work.

3. Look at areas of weakness

When – and only when – you have built up your confidence by identifying your strengths, consider your weaknesses and limitations, for example those imposed by family commitments. Be honest but positive. For every weakness you identify, think about ways of remedying it – through practice or training. Remember that no one in employment is perfect.

4. Identify opportunities

Relate your strengths to areas of job opportunity. Be creative in identifying options. Have new companies moved into the area or are they likely to? Use local sources of information such as libraries, directories and job centres.

5. Be honest about the barriers

Once you are clear about the opportunities, be honest at this stage about the potential barriers. These could include: travel, childcare, family resistance, lack of qualifications. Work through the list and be creative in thinking how each could be overcome, or be prepared to acknowledge that some will be insuperable. Enlist the help of family and friends at this stage.

6. Set goals and priorities that are right for you

Set clear goals for what you want to achieve from returning to work and take account of your own priorities rather than those of others. These could relate to finances, hours of work or type of employment. Be realistic with your targets: set ones that are achievable in the short to medium term rather than aiming too high initially.

7. Draw up an action plan which identifies simple steps

Take your goals and list the actions you need to take to achieve each one. Set yourself a realistic but stretching timetable and include dates against each action and a cost. Work out your overall timetable and budget and make any adjustments you need to.

8. Consider whether you need training to achieve your goals and identify the options

Will you need, or benefit from, training to achieve your goals? Consider all options, including:

- **a returner's course:** a short course to give you some preparation for work, probably including interview techniques and CV writing – this may be useful if you are returning to the same type of employment but need some confidence building

- **an updating course:** this is a longer version of the above, which may include the updating of skills such as word processing
- **further education or training leading to a qualification:** this will be more time-consuming, but will enable you to apply for a wider range of jobs
- **a course to help you acquire new skills:** so you can change career direction
- **a course to enable you to set up your own business.**

You can seek guidance on any of these options from:

- the **Educational Guidance Service** (a free local service aimed at adults; also called Education Shop, Learning Links or Educational Advice)
- the local **Job Centre**, which will provide advice on government training schemes and other retraining schemes in areas of skill shortage
- the local **Careers Office.**

9. Prepare yourself

If you have been away from work a long time, prepare yourself for returning by doing voluntary or committee work. Treat it as you would paid employment; learn from mistakes and experiences, and get used to working within time constraints.

10. Build your own networks

Consider joining a women returners' network or other local group of women in work. You will be able to share experience and develop new contacts – particularly useful if you are setting up your own business.

11. Begin searching for a job

Begin looking at advertised and non-advertised sources of employment: the local job centre, newspapers and free magazines, the Yellow Pages. Send your CV and a covering letter to all appropriate employers.

12. Draw up a CV

Draft a CV listing your education and qualifications, jobs to date and relevant skills and experience. Seek help from family, friends or the local careers adviser in refining the draft. Have the final version typed up.

13. Draw up a list of questions to ask employers

Focus on what is important to you, for example:

- subsidised childcare
- flexible leave arrangements to care for elderly or disabled relatives

- training to help you develop
- opportunities for promotion.

Dos and don'ts for an effective return to work

Do
- Be positive: take small steps initially to build your confidence.
- Get the support of your partner, family and relatives.

Don't
- Undertake extensive re-training or re-skilling before researching the local employment situation thoroughly: even training in an area of skill shortage may not guarantee you a job.

Useful reading
Back to work: a resource guide for women returners, Gill Sargeant, London: Industrial Society, 1995

Women mean business: a practical guide for women returners, Caroline Bamford and Catherine McCarthy, London: BBC Books, 1991

Returning to work: a directory of education and training for women, London: Kogan Page, 1990

Getting there: job hunting for women, 2nd ed, Margaret Wallis, London: Kogan Page, 1990

Returning to work: a practical guide for women, Alec Reed, London: Kogan Page, 1989

Useful addresses
Women Returners Network, 8 John Adam Street, London, WC2N 6EZ, Tel: 0171 839 8188

Industrial Society, Robert Hyde House, 48 Bryanston Square, London, W1H 7LN, Tel: 0171 262 2401

TRAINING AND ENTERPRISE COUNCILS (TECs)
Contact your local TEC for information about their training services and other re-training opportunities in your area.

Thought starters

- Where would you like to see yourself in 10 years' time? Will the goals you have set allow you to get there?
- What is your **real** priority in returning to work? Will your chosen route deliver this?
- What barriers are in your way? List them.
- How can you overcome these barriers?
- What would you do if you knew you could not fail?

Working Out a Career Plan

> **This checklist is designed for those embarking on planning and managing their careers.**

MCI Standards

This checklist has relevance for the MCI Management Standards: Key Role C – Manage People.

Definition

Career planning is in itself a straightforward process of understanding, exploring and decision making, reflecting on your life, family and work in a wider context. What complicates it is that careers and organisations are constantly changing. Careers have been defined as 'a set of improvisations based on loose assumptions about the future'.

Advantages of career planning

- Understanding yourself. Time spent on reflection is never wasted, as everyone has a unique mix of skills, strengths and limitations which change over time.
- Clarity – so that when opportunities emerge you are able to make informed choices.
- Monitoring. A realistic and achievable plan helps you to gauge your progress.

Disadvantages of career planning

There are no real disadvantages to planning your career – the only disadvantages arise if you plan badly.

- Practicality. Often people have unrealistic aspirations. Be sure to check them out with other people – colleagues, mentors, family and friends.

- Limited range – it is possible to view oneself as only ever occupying one type of job, and this can narrow career ambitions dramatically.
- Inflexibility: over-detailed planning that leaves little or no scope for responding to changes in circumstances that will inevitably occur.

Action checklist

1. Who am I?

The foundations of any plans for the future are based on your understanding of who you are, what is important to you, your dreams and plans for the future. This understanding helps you to begin a process of decision making about the future. Some simple questions can help you reflect on your career:

- what has triggered your moves in the past?
- what are the significant influences on your life, and how have these affected your career?
- what are your skills?
- what do you see as your strengths?
- what are your limitations?
- what have been your successes and failures?
- what values underlie your life?
- what are your current obligations and commitments?
- are there talents in you that you feel are underdeveloped?
- do you feel in a rut of any kind?
- are your answers to the above an accurate reflection of you – how do others see you?

2. What do I want?

Once you have completed a review of where you are it is good to begin to focus on the future – where you see yourself going. You should not be restricted by the normal constraints of realism at this stage. Ask:

- where do you see yourself in the short, medium and long term?

3. What options do I have?

There are two basic options – to **Make Changes** or to **Make No Changes**. But there are more sub-options if, for example, you decide:

- to make a big change in one area
- to make a small change in one area
- to make several small changes
- to plan changes over quite a long period
- to make changes as soon as possible.

4. No change

At this stage, you may decide that you don't wish to make any changes to your life – it could be that your current life is matching up to your vision of your ideal life. Or, from reviewing your obligations and commitments, you may decide that this is not the right time to be making any changes, and that plans for the future should be deferred for a while. Whatever the reason for opting for 'no change', it should be a positive and conscious decision, rather than one arrived at from a feeling of '... but I have no choice!'

5. Change your current position

Within your current job, there are bound to be ways in which you can enhance what you are doing and so increase the satisfaction you gain from it. Here is a list of suggestions. Not all will be appropriate for you and there may well be others which you can add ...

- undertake a new project
- organise a visit to another department
- participate in a 'job swap'
- volunteer for new responsibilities
- look for alternative ways of doing things
- offer to coach new juniors
- negotiate for a redefinition of your job to include more stretch
- shadow a colleague
- investigate the options of part-time, job share, or flexible employment.

6. Changing yourself

The key to changing your situation may lie in changing yourself, for example by learning new skills or updating rusty ones, by setting more realistic expectations for yourself, by setting yourself more ambitious targets, or by re-examining old attitudes. Again, here are a few suggestions:

- attend a course or training programme
- undertake an external course of study
- encourage feedback
- seek advice from someone you respect
- consult a careers advisor.

7. Changing your job

Within any organisation there may be opportunities to find something nearer your 'ideal' job. However, given that we operate in the real world, it is worth bearing certain 'home truths' in mind when making career plans and thinking of creative solutions to ensure as close a match as possible between what you want and what is available.

- Can you identify gaps in your skills?
- Can you use your time constructively to update old skills or learn new ones?
- Can you polish up your interview techniques?
- Does your CV need revising?

There are no guarantees that the right job will become available at the right time or that you will be successful in your application. Don't limit yourself by only thinking about opportunities which offer promotion; it may be time to think about a sideways move to broaden your experience and to increase your job satisfaction. Looking internally for opportunities is not as simple as looking at internal vacancies. It could be useful to follow up contacts or establish new ones in the particular areas you are attracted to.

8. Updating your plan

As time goes on you will probably find that you overestimated some abilities and underestimated others, that you have discovered capacities you did not realise you had, that circumstances have made some skills redundant and others more important and so on. Your plan will need regular revision – you should go through the processes outlined here at least every three years.

Dos and don'ts for career planning

Do

- Apply your management skills to managing your career.
- Audit where you are now.
- Evaluate how you can fill the gaps.
- Ask for feedback.
- Think about the changes necessary.
- Talk to others, develop your network.
- Update your career plan regularly.

Don't

- Depend on others recognising your potential.
- Devolve responsibility for your career on to your organisation.
- Take silly risks – you should be making informed choices.

Useful reading

Successful career planning in a week, 2nd ed, Wendy Hirsh and Charles Jackson, London: Hodder & Stoughton, 1998

Positioning for the unknown: career development for professionals in the 1990s, Jeff Watkins and Lynn Drury, Bristol: University of Bristol, 1994

Roads to the top, Ruth Tait, London: Macmillan, 1995

The career decisions planner, Joan Lloyd, Chichester: John Wiley, 1992

The perfect career, Max Eggert, London: Arrow Books, 1994

Useful addresses

Career Development Department, **Institute of Management,** Management House, Cottingham Road, Corby, Northants, NN17 1TT, Tel: 01536 204222

Thought starters

- It has never been as important as it is today to manage your career. Never devolve this responsibility to anyone else, as it is central to your well-being.
- It's not the most qualified people who get the best jobs – it's those who are most skilled at managing their careers and finding opportunities.
- Getting the perfect job is a job in itself.

Starting a New Job

> This checklist deals with steps which may usefully be taken by an indi-
> vidual prior to starting a new job and during the first few days in the
> job. Starting a new job does not begin on the first day with your new
> employer but before you even leave your current one. This checklist is
> also of relevance to organisations employing new starters.

MCI Standards

This checklist has relevance for the MCI Management Standards: Key Role
C – Manage People.

Definition

'Starting a new job' may imply that:

- an existing employee has been appointed to fill a vacancy in an existing
  or newly created job
- an individual has joined an organisation to fill a vacancy in an existing
  job or to assume the responsibilities of a newly created job.

The problems of the individual joining an organisation to start a new job
may generally be assumed to be greater than those of the individual who is
promoted or transferred within an organisation. This checklist therefore
focuses on the former situation.

Benefits of planning an approach to starting a new job

Planning:

- leads to reduced stress
- enables you to become productive more quickly
- enables you to become accepted by new colleagues more quickly 'as one
  of us'
- prepares you for the cultural changes and variations which often go with
  a new situation
- significantly reduces the potential for embarrassment which can arise in a
  new situation.

Action checklist

1. Act positively before you leave your present job

Sort out personnel issues, such as pension, private health insurance and your P45. Hand back company property, such as badges and passes.

Will you be required to repay some or all of the funding for qualifications? Are there any restrictions on your movements or actions in the future?

2. Reconcile the demands, actual and potential, of the new job with your private life

Recognise that, whatever the level of the job, there will be a period during which you are 'settling in', a period in which you will require both extra concentration and positive support. Recognise that the contexts of your private and working lives will both change and that it is preferable that the changes are discussed with your partner or family before they occur as they will affect them too.

3. Research the background of a new employer

Recognise that the more you know about the new employer the easier it will be for you during the initial period after you have joined the organisation. Expand on the research you will – or should – have carried out prior to your interview.

If you don't already have a copy of the new employer's annual report, obtain one. Identify:

- your new employer's competitors
- their relative degree of success or failure
- the basis on which they compete (such as price, quality, or service) or are protected from competition (because of location or access to raw materials for example).

Find out anything you can about the culture of the organisation, the people with whom you will be working, the structure within which they work and the reputation of the unit which you will be joining. Talk to people whom you know and who are already employed there.

If you are new to the industrial sector, consider how you can best familiarise yourself with it and acquire some familiarity with the terminology used in that sector. Remember that the people with whom you will be working may assume that you have the same degree of familiarity with their jargon as they have. Try to get abreast of the game.

Arm yourself with as much information as you can obtain in advance. Remember this process must continue after joining the organisation.

Consider what you have discovered and its implications for a newcomer. Identify what you still need to know and plan to obtain this information systematically and quickly after you have started your new job. Resolve not to acquire this information on a piecemeal basis, but to go after it – you will gain the advantages that knowledge brings and you will also impress your superiors and colleagues with your willingness to work and learn.

4. Discover the background if your new job is newly created

Seek to find out if, and why, the job was created, or if it merely fills a vacancy – and if so why the previous incumbent left. Was it to solve a problem and if so what was the problem? Was it to cope with expansion in activity and if so, what caused that expansion? Find out the structural context of the newly created job, future plans for it and, most of all, any special expectations of you as the newly appointed jobholder. Is the job unique in the organisation or are there others like it? Try to identify what characteristics and skills you are bringing to the job which made you the best person for it. Recognise that the demonstration of those characteristics and the deployment of those skills will almost certainly provide the criteria against which your performance will be judged.

5. Add to any knowledge you already have about the job

The induction programme organised by your new employer should provide you with information on your job and general background. If the information is not provided, you will need to ask or search for it. Recognise that you need to know:

- the purpose of the unit you have joined
- the purpose of your new job
- your responsibilities
- your authority
- the structure of the unit
- the unit's place in the structure of the organisation
- to whom you report and your boss's requirements
- who, if anyone, reports to you
- as much as possible about the culture and values of the unit and of the organisation
- whether relationships are formal or informal – does this apply to all of them?

Make sure you are clear on practical matters, such as:

- starting and finishing times (formal and real)
- coffee, tea and lunch arrangements
- the use of the telephone for private calls
- performance appraisal

- pensions
- private health care
- the position on unions
- funding for qualifications
- dress (formal or informal).

Recognise that what you need to know may range from the obviously important to the apparently trivial but, if it helps you 'fit in', become accepted and begin to achieve the purpose of your new job more quickly, it is worth knowing – 'trivial' aspects are often integral to the organisation's culture. Remember this may apply even more if you have been appointed to a newly created job.

6. Decide what behaviour patterns are appropriate and pursue them

Remember that you are the new boy or girl and that your behaviour will be the focus of some attention, particularly if your new role requires you to manage or supervise others. Remember also that junior employees 'know' more than their seniors in terms of helping you to find your way around. Be yourself but leave yourself with some room for manoeuvre in the light of what you may discover over the first two or three weeks in your new job.

Keep your eyes open; you will notice things in the first few weeks that you will take for granted soon, and you have a chance to change some of them later. Ask about them if you wish to, but don't criticise them – yet!

Don't:

- form alliances too quickly
- fall into the trap of exchanging badinage with the unit's clown
- put yourself in a position from which you may wish to retract
- be over-assertive
- take the lead in discussions, formal or informal
- take on too much in an effort to fit in better
- be too quick to suggest a visit to the pub as this may be seen as presumptuous.

Reserve your position until you see the lie of the land. Remember that it is easier to go forward than it is to retract. Be polite to everyone, offer help where it is appropriate but, even in offering help, don't allow yourself to be over-assertive.

7. Be prepared for that bewildered feeling!

You will meet a lot of new people and have to learn many new processes, whether it be in the content of your job or getting used to a different photocopier. Most people don't feel fully comfortable in their new job for at least six months, so don't worry too much after only a couple of days!

Useful reading

BOOK

Making an impact in your new job: the first 30 days, Elwood N Chapman, London: Kogan Page, 1990

JOURNAL ARTICLE

Sink or swim, David Fisher, Jane Howe and Laura Heath, Directions, Jul 1994, pp15–17

Dos and don'ts when starting a new job

Do

- Spend as much time as possible preparing for your new job.
- Recognise that life is going to change and prepare yourself for it.
- Consider carefully what you can bring to the job which might distinguish you from others.
- Display a degree of humility.

Don't

- Boast about your previous achievements.
- Refer constantly to the outstanding qualities as an employer of the organisation you have chosen to leave.
- Keep referring to 'how we did it in my previous organisation'.
- Make comparisons between your former employer and your new one.
- Display arrogance, however confident you feel inside.
- Express opinions too quickly which you may regret.

Thought starters

- Recall some newcomers to your previous organisation(s). How did their behaviour affect you?
- Why should they respect me?
- They know the rules – I don't.
- 'Different' doesn't mean 'better' or 'worse' – it means different.

Personal Development Planning

This checklist promotes personal development planning (PDP) as a way of enabling a constructive approach to acquiring knowledge and skills throughout working life.

The accelerating pace of market and technological change, the growth of information, and the shifts in economic and competitive pressures are all imposing increasing demands on managers to renew their skills and capabilities.

Flatter organisation structures mean fewer promotion possibilities. Managers are increasingly more likely to be faced with a series of sideways moves within and between organisations rather than with steady upward progression. Managers can no longer rely on their initial training or qualifications to carry them through employment, or on their employer to provide everything they need to develop skills and experience – the old security, if it ever existed, has gone. Increasingly the manager will take responsibility for their own lifelong, continuing development – the bottom-line is that it is down to the individual. The new security consists of loyalty – not complacency – to oneself, to one's own skills and potential.

MCI Standards

This checklist has relevance for the MCI Management Standards: Key Role C – Manage People.

Definition

Development is a lifelong process of nurturing, shaping and improving an individual's skills, knowledge and interests to ensure their maximum effectiveness and adaptability, and to minimise the obsolescence of their skills and their chances of redundancy. It does not necessarily imply upward movement; rather, it is about enabling individuals to improve and use their full potential at each career stage.

A personal development plan results from establishing what you want to achieve or where you want to go, in the short- or long-term, and identifying the need for skills, knowledge or competence. It also helps to define the appropriate development to meet those perceived needs. Scheduling and timing is important but cannot be too regimented.

PDP is a cyclical process – you don't have to start at the beginning if you have already decided where you are going and what you need to do to get there. The following chart outlines the process.

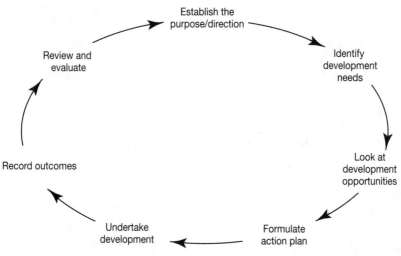

The Personal Development Planning Cycle

Benefits of PDP

Adopting a constructive approach to PDP provides a schedule to work to, facilitates motivation, and offers a framework for monitoring and evaluating achievements. It can lay the basis for:

- re-appraising where you want to go and how you can get there
- revitalising those technical skills that date very quickly
- building up transferable skills (such as self-awareness, ability to learn, adaptability to change, empathy, good time management)
- continuous learning
- gaining satisfaction from a sense of achievement
- helping to ensure employability and survival in an age where very few jobs can be guaranteed the same five years from now
- getting into a position where you can make the most of opportunities which may arise, or which you can make happen.

Problems with PDP

These are usually associated with:

- 'getting started' in a constructive way
- assigning importance to development activities which may not have seemed so important in the past

- being too modest, too demanding or perhaps too unrealistic
- getting the right balance between workaholism and inertia – between work, rest and play.

Action checklist

1. Establish the purpose or direction

The purpose of any development cycle needs to be identified. You may do this by yourself or with your manager, mentor, colleagues, or friends. It involves:

- gaining an awareness of your potential within your chosen sector
- gaining a measure of what you are good at and interested in
- taking account of the organisational realities you encounter and linking your plans to organisational needs as much as possible.

Think about:

- your own value system, involving private life and family, work and money, constraints and obstacles to mobility, now and in the future
- the characteristics of work that fit with your value system.

2. Identify development needs

The identification of development needs may emerge from intended or actual new tasks or responsibilities, from discussions with your manager or others, or from dissatisfaction with current routines. Some of us may know what we are good at, many of us may not. In order to find out, various instruments are available including self-assessment tests, benchmarking exercises against occupational standards, or personal diagnostics which elicit your view of yourself in a structured way.

Your development needs will differ depending on your career goals. If you intend to remain in similar employment, do you need development to re-motivate or re-orient yourself, or is the aim to improve your current performance and effectiveness? Or is development to prepare you for promotion, your next job, a new career or self-employment?

3. Identify learning opportunities

As a result of one, or several, of the assessment processes above, draw up a list of the skills or knowledge you will need to acquire, update or improve. Compare this list to your current skills and knowledge base and identify the gaps. Consider:

- **your learning style** – some of us learn best from trying new things, whilst others prefer to sit back and observe; some prefer to put things to the test, others to carry out research at first or second hand. Honey and Mumford have devised an instrument to help you identify your preferred learning style.

- **the resources available** – think laterally when trying to identify sources of help for development. In addition to your own organisation, consider government and private advisory agencies, literature and open learning aids, multi-media packages, professional institutes, your peer groups, networks and colleagues and from family and friends.

- **the range of learning options available**. These can be broadly differentiated into three categories.

  - **Education** takes place over a sustained but finite period of time, usually leads to a qualification and may result in leading you to a new career direction.
  - **Training** takes place at a specific time and place, is usually vocationally relevant and limited to specific aims and objectives which can be measured.
  - **Development** encompasses a large number of activities which offer learning potential but which are neither education nor course-based, rather work-based (such as work shadowing, job rotation, secondment, attachment, mentoring,delegation, counselling, or coaching) or personal (such as private reading, authorship, presenting papers, peer group contacts, networking, or community involvement).

4. Formulate an action plan

For each of the gaps you have identified, set yourself development objectives. These need to be SMART: Specific, Measurable, Achievable, Realistic and Timely. There must be an element of challenge in them so they stretch you as an individual and carry you on to new ground. But they must also be attainable and viable within a realistic time-frame, otherwise time will overtake you.

5. Undertake the development

Put your plan into action – your development is up to you.

6. Record the outcomes

Keeping records serves to remind you – and others such as potential employers – of what you have done. Most importantly they help you to focus on what you have got out of the development activity. Record the date, the development need identified, the chosen method of development, the date(s) that development was undertaken, the outcomes, and further action.

7. Evaluate and review

Evaluation is the key stage to the self-development cycle because it enables you to discover whether that development activity was worthwhile, applicable, and if and how your skills or working behaviour improved as a result. Evaluating development activities involves asking:

- what am I better able to do as a result?
- has this experience thrown up further development needs?
- how well did this development method work?
- could I have gained more from this activity?
- would I follow this approach again?

Evaluation will also provide a key lead to the next stage of the continuing cycle.

Goals change, tasks vary and new needs will emerge. It is important to revise your own plan accordingly. A plan that does not evolve and adapt is probably not being followed.

Dos and don'ts for personal development planning

Do

- Make sure your personal goals are balanced.
- Take time to reflect on and evaluate learning experiences.
- Seek out feedback on your performance.
- Focus on development in two different directions at the same time:
  - for specific goals or careers
  - for greater flexibility and adaptability to changing circumstances.

Don't

- Be too ambitious; development is usually incremental.
- Be afraid of asking for help.

Useful reading

Manual of learning styles, Peter Honey and Alan Mumford, Maidenhead: Peter Honey Publications, 1982
Test your management skills: the management self-assessment test, Corby: Institute of Management, 1995
Career paths for the 21st Century: how to beat job insecurity, Jim Durcan and David Oates, London: Century Business, 1996

Thought starters

- There were two stone-cutters chipping away in a quarry. Asked what they were doing, one said: 'I'm cutting stone.' The other said: 'I'm building a cathedral'. (**Past tense, future perfect**, Malcolm Kerrell, London. Souvenir Press, 1996, p. 127)
- 'All men who have turned out worth anything have had the chief hand in their own education.' (Sir Walter Scott, 1830)

Marketing Yourself

This checklist provides outline guidance and advice on how to market yourself.

Whatever you are selling – cars, perfume, refreshments, finance or your own skills and talents – to an employer or customer, the principles of sales and marketing remain the same. It won't do any good to be strong, confident, skilled and qualified if you keep it a secret. If you want to be successful, you are going to have to let the rest of the world know about yourself.

MCI Standards

This checklist has relevance for the MCI Management Standards: Key Role C – Manage People.

Definition

Marketing theory focuses the organisation's or individual's attention on the perceived needs and wants of the marketplace. Philip Kotler has defined marketing as a human activity directed at satisfying needs and wants through exchange processes.

For the purposes of this checklist the exchange processes comprise skills, techniques, abilities, competence and image, and they take place between (potential) employer and employee, or between customer and supplier.

Action checklist

1. Familiarise yourself with the product

Marketing yourself starts with knowing yourself. You need to know what the product is, what its strengths and weaknesses are, what opportunities and threats there are around, what image the package is projecting, who the product is directed at, who is going to buy it and how to renew and refresh it once shelf-life approaches its limit and obsolescence sets in.

Look at yourself objectively to identify your skills and qualities. Try to imagine yourself as if you were an external observer. Observe yourself entering a room, think of the impression you make and what you would want to change.

2. Be aware of the product's inherent strengths and weaknesses

Be aware of:

- how well you can motivate and negotiate
- how well you manage your time and keep your promises to others
- how well you cope under pressure
- how often you put off difficult tasks
- how effective you are working on your own or as part of a team
- how flexible and adaptable you are to new challenges and what kind of reaction you will have to forthcoming changes
- how you learn best, and least well – whether you like to get on with things, try them and learn as you go, or whether you prefer to hold back, reflect and think things through before getting involved
- whether you are at the peak, trough or in the middle of a learning curve, whether you know what you want to tackle next, or whether you are plateaued – albeit temporarily.

3. List product features and benefits

People often describe themselves solely in terms of what they are. Talking in terms of benefits means adding how these aspects of yourself will benefit the customer/employer. For example, a willingness to take on responsibility (feature) implies capability to accept more delegated tasks (benefit to employer):

Feature	Benefit
Punctual, reliable	Consistency
Delivers on time	Trustworthiness
Diligent, productive	Cost-effectiveness
Ambitious	Drive and energy

4. Be aware of product stereotypes

Some jobs are characterised by high turnover (retail, publishing), others as universally 'solid' (accounting, banking), some as exciting and attractive (media, travel), others as intellectual and 'clever' (lecturing, journalism). However wrong the stereotype in reality, bear in mind that people's traditional perceptions will influence their perception of you. Just think of the image accountants or librarians have!

5. Ensure the quality processes

To improve product quality, you must learn from your mistakes. Learning to learn from mistakes is an important part of the quality and marketing processes. It helps you to build confidence in yourself and, in turn, others will have confidence in you. Self-confidence is a necessary prerequisite to self-marketing. The contrary is also true: when you don't believe in yourself, you are only selling yourself short.

6. Work on product image

You have an image whether you like it, plan it or not, so you might as well make the best of it.

Think of yourself as a brand name, a product in the marketplace. As you go through a working day, remember that everything you do, say and write, adds value to – or takes value from – your own 'brand' image.

Recognise that the way you interact with people probably varies from individual to individual; think of what leaves you and them satisfied or dissatisfied, confused or focused. Remember that too much self-deprecation can be as negative as too much self-importance.

7. Review product packaging

Whenever you can, use good design to present to the world the image that will do the most for you. This does not mean turning yourself into a film star; rather work at things that improve your image and come reasonably easily to you. It may be your notepaper, business card, the way you present a report, how you communicate to groups, the layout of your office, or even just the way you dress.

Before you leave for work tomorrow take a look in the mirror and ask yourself what your clothes tell other people about you. You can be sure that your clothes convey some kind of image, intended or not, so at least be aware of it. Decide if you want to do anything about it. Remember – more than half the image you create is in the way you look.

Your voice is as important as the way you look, and its tone, inflection and accent can inspire confidence – or the opposite – without your knowing or intending it. What mood does your voice convey? Are there things you want to change? If necessary get professional help. It's not so much what you say but the way that you say it that counts.

Watch your body language – how you walk, whether you constantly fidget with your hands, whether you frown a lot, whether you look directly at people when you talk to them. Learn to relax when the going gets tough – it gives the impression that you are on top of the situation.

Consult friends as to how you are coming across – the odds are that you will be very surprised, quite probably pleasantly so. Remember it is impossible for us to see ourselves as others see us – so find out how others do! If your self-image is badly in conflict with the image others have of you, efforts to market yourself may end in disaster.

8. Create product awareness

Get yourself, your name and your face known. This can be achieved by:

- extending your contacts
- getting involved
- organising
- writing articles
- doing committee work
- speaking up at meetings
- volunteering new ideas
- taking risks
- finding a mentor
- believing in yourself
- being memorable – as long as it is positive.

Be aware too that it is possible to over-cook the goose – too much exposure is as dangerous as not enough.

9. Promote the product

Make a list of the people or categories of people who need to know about you in order for your skills to be further exploited, or for the profitability of your business to increase, or for you to make the next move in your career.

Accurate targeting is a vital ingredient and more rewarding than the scatter-gun shot in the dark. Give it all the time you can by identifying the profile of your best customer – it should help to identify the profile of your best prospect.

10. Set product targets

Sometimes we are afraid to set challenging goals because they seem distant and unreachable. Break down daunting processes into small, achievable steps. Make them SMART – specific, measurable, attainable, realistic and time-scheduled. Don't think of yourself starting from Point A and magically arriving at Point Z; instead envisage yourself going through each step, concentrating on getting the detail right, learning from mistakes, and enjoying the fact that you are making progress.

Dos and don'ts for marketing yourself

Do
- Take a positive attitude.
- Believe in yourself.
- Try to increase your visibility.
- Review your image.

- Be enthusiastic about your work.
- Seek professional help and advice where necessary.
- Network as much as possible.
- Make the most of opportunities.
- Capitalise on your strengths and make them work for you.

Don't
- Be afraid to make changes.
- Be negative about yourself.
- Be over-modest about your achievements.
- Hide yourself away.
- Ignore the value of personal contacts.

Useful reading

Sell yourself: persuasive tactics to boost your image, Polly Bird, London: Pitman Publishing, 1994

Marketing yourself: how to sell yourself and get the jobs you've always wanted, Dorothy Leeds, London: Guild Publishing, 1991

Personal power – how to achieve influence and success in your professional life, Philippa Davies, London: Piatkus, 1991

Springboard: women's development workbook, Liz Willis and Jenny Daisley, Stroud: Hawthorn Press, 1990

Thought starters

- Research by Harvey Coleman shows that there are three factors that are used to judge an individual, or determine whether someone is promoted or not:

Performance	10%
Image	30%
Exposure	60%

  (Willis and Daisley)

- There are four kinds of people in the world:
  - People who watch things happen
  - People to whom things happen
  - People who don't know what is happening
  - People who make things happen.

- It is no use marketing inferior products – make sure you are worth marketing!

Succeeding as a New Manager

This checklist examines the situation facing a newly appointed manager, whose new job is more demanding than the previous one.

MCI Standards

This checklist has relevance for the MCI Management Standards: Key Role C – Manage People.

Definition

A 'new manager' is the newly appointed holder of a post where the incumbent has responsibility for a team of no more than 12–15 subordinates. The relationship between the manager and the team is a new one, although the manager:

- may previously have been a member of the team or a manager in another part of the same organisation
- may be experiencing the responsibilities of managing at this level for the first time, or indeed of managing at all for the first time.

The range of possible previous experience is wide, but the principles outlined here apply to any 'new manager'.

Action checklist

1. Get it right before you start

When you have recovered from the euphoria of your new appointment, settle down and recognise that, at least for a period, you will be in a more demanding situation than before. Face the fact that, even when you have got to grips with your new role, life may continue to be more demanding than it has ever been before.

Recognise that you will need two things at home – support during a period in which you will be subjected to a degree of stress, and a lack of distraction to enable you to focus single-mindedly on your new responsibilities. From the earliest possible moment discuss and continue to discuss any likely implications of the change in your position on your relationships with your partner and family, and on the pattern of life which you have developed together.

2. Learn about the job in advance

Find out all you can about:

- the company (if it is one you have not previously worked for)
- the unit where you will work within the company
- your new job itself
- the history of the position
- your new subordinates if you don't already know them.

Accumulate information and find out as much as you can about your predecessor and their approach to the job – but don't make assumptions without facts, and remember that your knowledge will still be incomplete. Establish:

- why they left
- what their management style was
- what needs to be changed in the job.

Take a view on what you want to achieve, on how you propose to develop yourself to match the demands of the job, and of the future. Reflect on your strengths and weaknesses – how can you deploy your positive characteristics to advantage and compensate for less strong points? Don't assume your new team will welcome your style – even if your predecessor was not popular with them, they may see unpleasant certainty being replaced by something they don't understand and are not ready for.

Form at least a tentative plan in advance, as it is difficult to plan once you are in post, but don't depart too dramatically and quickly from established practice.

A final thought about pre-planning: don't prejudge what you're going to find in your new job, or be hidebound by what you've done in previous jobs.

3. Make the most of your induction

On your first day you should be met by someone from the Personnel Department or perhaps your line manager, who will show you round, introduce you to other colleagues and attend to formalities. They will introduce you to your team (and your line manager if different). Be proactive in arranging your induction – is there anything you want to know about that has not been covered?

4. Get to know your team

Discover the purpose for which your department, team or unit exists – what is the state of play, what work is taking place, what are the expectations of 'customers' which you must satisfy?

If your new team is based in an office, ask someone to get them together, introduce yourself, say just a few words about yourself, and tell them you are looking forward to working with them. Tell them you'll see them all individually as quickly as possible. (If they are not based in an office but scattered, aim to get them together quickly for the same purpose.)

Meet your team one by one. Allocate time for this purpose generously. Preferably plan in advance a framework within which your discussion will take place – with foresight you can have a 'spontaneous structured' exchange of information with a friendly but businesslike approach. Be courteous and listen carefully, but remember you want information about them as individuals and ensure you get it from them. Plan to take notes and explain why. Consider leaving them with a question to reflect on: 'What should I do or not do to help you carry out your job as effectively as possible?'

Evaluate your new team before you plan to augment it.

If you are aware that another team member wanted or expected to get your job, broach the subject to get it out into the open. Don't be patronising, but express the hope that you can work together on a friendly basis. Say that you look forward to his or her help. Be careful – the team have a yardstick against which to measure you. And be especially careful if the rest of the team think the person in question should have got the job.

5. Develop relationships inside and outside your organisation

Introduce yourself to customers (internal as well as external), suppliers and as many as possible of those who make up the network in which your job takes place. Begin to develop a relationship with your boss but not too quickly. Find out how close they want you to be. Don't make the mistake of encouraging a close working relationship until you have finished your reconnaissance.

6. Identify criteria against which you expect to be judged

Observe, listen and note what is acceptable and what is not acceptable in the environment you have entered. You should know within a few weeks what your staff expect of you. Identify the criteria by which your boss, your peers and your 'customers' (internal or external) will judge you. Be honest with yourself – can you match those criteria and, if not, what must you do to ensure that you can? Consider carefully who could help you and what the price might be.

7. Work on your relationship with individuals

Follow up your initial meetings when they have all been completed. Respect the hierarchy but don't let this stop you from beginning the process of developing individuals to realise their full potential. Remember to notice and show appreciation when extra time and effort are put in. Tell people about their good points and foster self-belief.

Set yourself a 'code of practice' for the management of individuals, covering individuals' development and progress. Make the code known but recognise that you will be judged by the extent to which you carry out the promises you have made. Include in the code the intention:

- to listen to what staff are saying
- to help staff develop specific plans to improve their performance
- to establish clear and specific goals and standards for individuals
- to help individuals understand how their jobs contribute to team effectiveness
- to ensure that each individual's duties and responsibilities are clearly understood
- to discuss performance honestly and directly; to give regular feedback on performance; to work hard to reach mutual agreement on performance appraisal; to consider all relevant information when evaluating performances; and to ensure that performance appraisal is consistent with informal feedback
- to provide training and guidance to improve performance and a basis for further development
- to sit down with individuals at least once a quarter
- to discuss overall performance.

8. Set out to develop a winning team

Teamworking is gradually becoming more accepted but even in those organisations where it is not the norm, the good practice behind the principles may still be implemented.

Research has demonstrated many times that good people management and good results are closely related. Recognise that you will be judged by your team's results.

Lead by involving team members. Make the maximum effort, as early as possible, to establish departmental and group goals. Seek the participation of your new staff in deciding the priority of goals and objectives and in setting deadlines for goals. Give your staff an opportunity to influence performance goals and standards: establish clear and specific goals and standards.

Set an example. Demonstrate strong personal commitment to the achievement of the team's goals. Communicate high personal standards informally, in conversation, in appearance and in your conduct generally. Build warm, friendly relationships rather than remaining cold and aloof.

9. Take stock regularly

At the end of your first week as a new manager take time to reflect on the progress you have made; on those things to which you must pay attention; and on any mistakes you have made. Don't let the identification of mistakes be the occasion for self-doubt. Everyone makes mistakes; good managers learn from them, bad managers repeat them. Make a plan for the following week and repeat this process weekly.

The new manager has to listen and learn, but not for too long; the pattern of behaviour set in the first three months will be extremely hard to change thereafter.

Dos and don'ts for succeeding as a new manager

Do
- Make your highest priority the development of your new staff.
- Use all the time at your disposal, before assuming your new role, to prepare for it.
- Leave yourself with room to manoeuvre by not taking up rigid positions prematurely.
- Recognise that first impressions of people may be replaced by more realistic ones.

Don't
- Make promises which may be unnecessary, or difficult or impossible to keep.
- Make alliances based on first impressions.
- Allow yourself to be trapped into accepting the status quo – reserve the right to postpone judgement.

Useful reading

The first time manager, 2nd ed, M J Morris, London: Kogan Page, 1994

Successful boss's first 100 days: the official guide for the new boss, Richard Koch, London: Pitman in association with the Institute of Management, 1994

New manager's handbook: a reference guide to the best in management practice, Michael Armstrong, London: Kogan Page, 1990

The new manager, Alfred Tack, Aldershot: Gower, 1988

The new manager's survival manual: all the skills you need for success, Clay Carr, New York: John Wiley, 1989

The new manager, Mike Woods, Shaftesbury: Element Books, 1988

Thought starters

- Have you defined your objectives? Do they need to be reviewed?
- What do you expect from a new boss?
- Which new bosses have impressed you most and why?

Effective Communications: Preparing Presentations

This checklist is intended for those who are required to give any form of presentation. It covers all the stages of preparing a talk, from accepting the invitation to checking the venue: the delivery of the presentation itself is covered in the following checklist (see Effective Communications: Delivering Presentations). This checklist concentrates on how to develop an effective personal style rather than on the preparation of visual aids.

MCI Standards

This checklist has relevance for the MCI Management Standards: Key Role D – Manage Information.

Definition

For the purposes of this checklist, a presentation covers any talk to a group, whether formal or informal, from giving a team briefing to delivering a major speech: the same rules and principles apply.

Action checklist

1. Decide whether to accept

Ask yourself whether you are the right person to deliver this presentation. Do you have enough time to prepare? You may need to allow between 30 and 60 minutes for every minute of delivery. Are you excited enough about the topic to be enthusiastic? Do you know enough to answer awkward questions? If not, say no!

2. Clarify the details

Find out how long you will speak for and the exact subject. Will there be questions at the end? If there are other speakers, what will they cover, and how will you fit in with them?

3. Research your audience

View the audience as your customers. Try to gain a notion of their expectations: do they want to be informed, amused or challenged? How many will there be; what is their level and background; do they have any prior knowledge?

4. Define the purpose

Tailor the presentation to meet the audience needs you identified. Is the aim of the presentation to:

- persuade – a sales pitch
- instruct – if you know your topic
- inspire – as part of a change programme
- entertain – if you are naturally funny.

5. Assemble your material

Assemble anything relevant to your topic: ideas; articles; quotes; anecdotes; references. Accumulate the material over time but don't attempt to organise it while you collect it.

6. Organise your material

Review your collection. Group items into themes and topics. Are there metaphors or analogies which keep appearing?

7. Prepare an 'essay plan'

Structure the material into a rough plan. Aim for a beginning, a middle and an end.

8. Write a rough draft

Use the essay plan to sketch a first draft. Write without stopping and don't impose a structure while writing. Aim to tell the audience what you are going to say: tell them and end by summarising what you have told them. Try to make only five key points and a maximum of seven.

9. Edit the draft

Sleep on your first draft. Review it the following day. Convert the written word to speech: make the text more concrete, simpler and more illustrative. Use anecdotes. Shorten all your sentences and eliminate non-essential ideas and words. Cut any jargon or explain any that is unavoidable. Make sure the timing is right – speaking to an audience is slower than talking to a friend.

10. Refine the draft

Run through the draft several times, preferably in front of someone. Seek feedback and criticism on content, style and delivery. Ask your listener not to interrupt but to make notes.

11. Select your prompts

If you want or need to deliver a spontaneous presentation, run through the draft again and begin to highlight prompts – key words and phrases. These will be the basis of your script and perhaps your visual aids. Practise using the prompts alone and learn the thoughts behind the words. When you are confident, transfer the prompts to numbered cards. Continue practising and reducing the number of key words. (Sometimes, you will need to use a full script, for example, if the press are present, or if the occasion is very formal).

12. Select appropriate presentation aids

Presentation aids need to:

- be integrated – flow from your natural style
- move the presentation on – add value to it and be clearly relevant to content, or summarise what you are saying thus dispensing with a script
- be professional – clear, readable and consistent
- be appropriate in tone – full colour slides may not be right for a small informal group
- be simple to understand – clearly legible from the back of the room
- be graphic where appropriate – use symbols, drawings and charts to reinforce your words.

An increasing range of presentation aids, from flip charts and overhead transparencies to multimedia and computer generated graphics, is available.

13. Rehearse

Practise in your head, in front of a mirror or in front of a partner – he or she will be your sternest critic! Note any mannerisms you need to correct or anything you need constantly to remind yourself of as you talk: 'Don't put your hands in pockets!'. 'Smile!'. Keep these on a cue card when you give the presentation.

14. Check the venue

Sit where the audience will sit and check your visuals are visible. Sit or stand where you will deliver the presentation and check you can work the equipment. Can you use the microphone?

Dos and don'ts for preparing effective presentations

Do

- Practise as much as possible. Seek feedback and be open to criticism.
- Constantly review the purpose of your presentation against the text: are you meeting the customer's expectations?
- Remember that thorough preparation is a key factor in minimising nerves and ensuring a successful presentation.
- Put some enthusiasm into your presentation – stimulate the audience.

Don't

- Sit in a room with a blank sheet of paper and try to write: look for external stimuli.
- Use a visual aid just because it is funny or striking and you can't bear to leave it out.
- Take anything for granted: the topic; the audience; the extent of their knowledge; the venue; the equipment.

Useful reading

Successful presentation in a week, 2nd ed, Malcolm Peel, London: Hodder & Stoughton, 1998

I hate giving presentations: your essential confidence booster, Michael D Owen, Ely: Fenman, 1997

Making successful presentations, Patrick Forsyth, London: Sheldon Press, 1995

Successful presentations, Carole McKenzie, London: Century Business, 1993

The perfect presentation, Andrew Leigh and Michael Maynard, London: Century Business, 1993

Janner's complete speechmaker, 4th ed, Greville Janner QC MP, London: Business Books Ltd UK, 1991

Thought starters

- Have you agreed to speak just because you were asked: if so, do you really know and care enough about the topic to excite your audience?
- Are you trying to convey too much information in one presentation? Your audience will only absorb a maximum of seven key points.

Effective Communications: Delivering Presentations

This checklist is intended for anyone giving a presentation, whether formal or informal. It assumes that you have spent time in preparing an effective presentation (see the previous checklist, Effective Communications: Preparing Presentations) and are now ready to deliver it.

MCI Standards

This checklist has relevance for the MCI Management Standards: Key Role D – Manage Information.

Definition

For the purposes of this checklist, a presentation covers any talk to a group, whether formal or informal, from giving a team briefing to delivering a major speech: the same rules and principles apply.

Action checklist

1. Choose the right style

The size of your audience and the purpose of the presentation will determine its style. Obtain precise information about audience size: a large audience for one presenter is but a small group to another.

- For five to ten, aim for an informal style with few visual aids. Sit or balance on the edge of a table or desk. Plan to establish relationships immediately and engage each individual.
- For ten to thirty, you need a more formal style but you can still establish relationships. Stand up and expect to use some visual aids.
- For thirty to a hundred, you will need good presentation aids and a formal style; it will be difficult to engage with individuals.

- Over a hundred, view this as a theatre style presentation: you will be 'on stage' and performing with a microphone. Your facial gestures and body language will need to be exaggerated to be effective.

2. Check the venue

Do a last minute check on equipment: can you use the microphone, the projector, are your visual aids visible? Who will introduce you and when? Is there a glass of water to hand?

3. Check your appearance

Ensure your appearance doesn't detract from your message. Dress conservatively and tidily. Check your tie, shoes, make-up.

4. Establish your presence

Once you have been introduced, pause; take a deep breath; look at the audience; make eye contact and acknowledge their presence. Relax your body and stand tall. Smile!

5. Establish your credentials

Explain why you are there and what gives you the authority to speak. Confirm the audience's expectations by announcing what you will speak about. Resolve any confusions or queries immediately: it is always possible you are in the wrong place!

6. Involve your audience

Get their attention initially using a visual aid or something unexpected. Ask a question, even if it is rhetorical. Say something that shows you understand their concerns or expectations. Deflecting attention to the audience removes some of the attention from you and helps with stage fright.

7. Let your personality show

Remember that feelings, not facts, convince people. Put genuine conviction behind what you are saying and allow your emotions to show through. This will also help you to overcome stage fright.

8. Use positive body language

Remember to stand erect. Don't lean on the lectern and don't play with your hair, tie, jewellery or clothing. For those who talk better on the move, walk around naturally and use your hands as you would in conversation for emphasis. Use ordinary facial expressions and, where appropriate, smile!

9. Take control of your voice

Project your voice through standing straight and breathing deeply. Speak clearly and more slowly than usual. Speak naturally but lower the pitch of your voice if you are nervous. Be aware of your speech mannerisms and consciously avoid repeating them. Avoid hesitating: if you have lost your place or your nerve, just pause, but don't 'um' or 'er'.

10. Introduce variety

Vary the timing of your delivery and the pitch of your voice. Speed up or slow down and change tone in different sections. Use inflections and emphases even if they sound exaggerated to you. Occasionally pause or stop completely in a long presentation – the audience need time to absorb the content and you need time to reflect: are you going too quickly; have you put your hands in your pockets without realising it?

11. Build on your rapport with the audience

Maintain eye contact and play to the cheerleaders – people you know or sense to be sympathetic. Show how your presentation is relevant to them and avoid using 'I' or 'me' too often.

12. Introduce humour

If you are confident, use humour to lighten or vary the mood. Use it only to support the text, not in its own right. Don't be cruel to anyone in the audience.

13. Face up to the unexpected

The audience will notice disturbances or mistakes but you will only remember how you handled them. Acknowledge rather than ignore interruptions and try to deflect or make light of them through humour.

14. Improvise

Although thorough preparation is essential it may be inappropriate to come over as too 'prepared', slick or clinical. Remember to adjust to the mood and atmosphere of the audience.

15. Conclude

Bring the presentation to a conclusion. Be brief, don't repeat the main text and end on a high, in tone, energy and content. Leave the audience wanting slightly more.

16. Be positive about questions

Actively encourage questions. Repeat the question so everyone can hear it. If you don't know the answer, admit it but offer to take a name and address to reply to later. Don't get into debate or argument.

Dos and don'ts for delivering effective presentations

Do

- Be yourself: allow your own personality to come through rather than trying to emulate presenters you admire.
- Start and finish on time – or before time if there are to be questions – otherwise you will lose the audience's sympathy regardless of how good the content is.
- Use handouts to convey detailed or complex ideas rather than cramming them into your presentation.

Don't

- Try to cover too much in one presentation and end up rushing to finish by talking faster.
- Use humour inappropriately or use it against your audience: you are the only legitimate target in the room.
- Use too many visual aids: they distract the audience and rarely add value.

Useful reading

Successful presentation in a week, 2nd ed, Malcolm Peel, London: Hodder & Stoughton, 1998
I hate giving presentations: your essential confidence booster, Michael D Owen, Ely: Fenman, 1997
Making successful presentations, Patrick Forsyth, London: Sheldon Press, 1995
The perfect presentation, Andrew Leigh and Michael Maynard, London: Century Business, 1993
Successful presentations, Carole McKenzie, London: Century Business, 1993
Janner's complete speechmaker, 4th ed, Greville Janner QC MP, London: Business Books Ltd, 1991

Thought starters

- Does each part of the content of your speech match up to the title and purpose?
- Do all your visual aids really add something to the spoken word?
- Have you tried your presentation out on guinea pigs for length, humour or interest?
- Have you ever used the particular visual aid you will be working with before?
- Do you know who your audience will be or how many there will be?

Stress Management: Self First

This checklist is designed to help individuals recognise symptoms of stress and sources of pressure and identify coping strategies.

Successive waves of downsizing, closures and reorganisations put pressure on managers and employees alike. Additionally, technological changes to improve the speed of communications in the form of fax machines, mobile telephones and e-mail have created twenty-four hour accessibility. This is a potential recipe for disaster. The detrimental effects of poorly managed pressures can be measured in terms of the cost to organisations and society as a whole. It has been estimated that 40 million working days or £7 billion are lost annually due to stress. The cost to individuals is less easy to measure but it affects the quality of life and relationships and can be enormous.

MCI Standards

This checklist has relevance for the MCI Management Standards: Key Role C – Manage People.

Definition

Stress has been defined as 'an excess of perceived demands over an individual's perceived ability to meet them' (JM Atkinson).

Studies have shown that stress is closely related to the degree of control an individual has over their work – self-controlled pressure can be tolerated at a very high level, while the threshold for imposed pressure is low. The experience of stress therefore is very personal. Pressures come from many different directions, affecting us in different ways at different times. In some situations when we are under an enormous amount of pressure, we cope, are stimulated and on occasion positively thrive. In other situations we may suffer in some way, show signs of not coping and feel unable to meet either the deadlines or the expectations – this is the experience of stress. Most people need a certain level of pressure to motivate them – it is when it gets beyond this level that problems arise.

Action checklist

1. Recognise your symptoms

Symptoms can alert you to the fact that you may be under stress. Commonly experienced symptoms include:

Health
- headaches, upset stomach, sleep problems, change in appetite, tense muscles, indigestion, exhaustion, stomach, intestinal and skin problems, and heart attacks.

Behaviour
- feeling worried, irritated, demotivated, unable to cope and make decisions, being less creative, nail biting, excessive smoking and/or use of alcohol.

Work
- lower job satisfaction, communication breakdown and a focus on unproductive tasks.

All these symptoms may be experienced in normal life; they only become symptoms of stress when several occur together, when they do not have an obvious cause, or when you experience them more often than you would expect. Also, whilst the symptoms are often exhibited in your workplace behaviour, they are not necessarily a reflection of workplace pressures.

2. Identify the sources

We live in an ever-changing world and must constantly adapt and adjust to technological and social changes. In addition, there are recurring pressures which form a predictable pattern of events in our lives, which can be a source of stress and satisfaction.

In everyday life these may include:

- death of someone close
- divorce
- injury
- moving house
- a large mortgage
- holidays
- birth of a child (especially the first).

In work they may include:

- time pressures
- demanding deadlines
- relationships with others

- too much or too little work
- business or work changes
- threat of redundancy
- pressure from above
- insensitive management.

3. Know your response

Individuals respond to these external pressures by adapting and adjusting in a variety of ways, depending on their lifestyle. Two broad categories have been identified according to personality type. Type 'A' people could be described as competitive, aggressive or hasty, whilst Type 'B' people are just the reverse. Type 'A' people tend to take stress out on others, Type 'B' to internalise it. Other characteristics such as age, gender, health, financial situation and access to support can influence how we respond to change, regardless of our personality traits.

4. Identify the strategies which help you cope

As individuals react differently to stress, so each one has different coping strategies. Identify for yourself those that have been successful in the past; they may have involved:

- removing or reducing the outside pressure
- accepting the things that can't be changed
- breaking up 'big' problems into smaller, achievable goals.

5. Begin to make the necessary changes

Change yourself – we can be our own worst enemies:

- be realistic
- recognise your own weaknesses
- learn to say 'no'
- talk to others, at home and at work: do not bottle up stress
- remember you are not the only one who is stressed: you are not alone.

Change relationships – relationships can be both supportive and damaging:

- invest in developmental and supportive relationships
- withdraw from damaging relationships.

Change activities – activities create balance and an opportunity for release:

- relax, if necessary by using well established techniques
- develop interests that nourish you
- take sensible exercise – a great way to relieve tension
- eat well; eat a sensibly balanced diet
- get enough sleep to ensure you are refreshed.

Your happiness and well-being depend on making changes. When change comes, it will bring with it an easing of pressures, profound changes in personality and mood and an approach to life which benefits you and those with whom you live and work.

Dos and don'ts for managing stress

Do
- Recognise your symptoms and warning signs.
- Identify the sources of pressure.
- Accept yourself as you are.
- Pace yourself; complete tasks rather than juggling 'all the balls in the air'.
- Forget the near misses.
- Communicate effectively; this can save time and energy.
- Remove or reduce outside pressures.
- Take a break: don't be afraid to relax – it is essential to regain your energy.
- Treat yourself occasionally.
- Look after your health and learn relaxation techniques.
- Talk to others.

Don't
- Think that stress equates with weakness.
- Keep it to yourself.
- Ignore it, thinking it will heal itself.
- Blame others or the environment.
- Stop activity completely – doing something else which you enjoy is more therapeutic than doing nothing, which gives time to worry.

Useful reading
Managing workplace stress, Susan Cartwright and Cary L Cooper, Thousand Oaks, California: Sage, 1997
How to manage stress for success, Sara Zeff Geber, New York: Amacom, 1996
Successful stress management in a week, Cary L Cooper and Alison Straw, London: Hodder & Stoughton, 1998
The stress workbook: how individuals, teams and organisations can balance pressure and performance, Eve Warren and others, London: Industrial Society, 1993
Stress and challenge at the top: the paradox of the successful executive, James C Quick and others, Chichester: John Wiley, 1990
Coping with stress at work, J M Atkinson, Wellingborough: Thorsons, 1988

Useful addresses
British Association of Counselling (Assn for Counselling at Work), 1 Regent Place, Rugby, Warwickshire, CV21 2PJ, Tel: 01788 578328

Thought starters

- How would you advise a subordinate who was under stress?
- Where do you invest most of your time and attention – do tasks or people matter most?
- Often our greatest enemy in looking after ourselves is ourselves – do you place unrealistic expectations on yourself? How could you prevent this?
- How much pressure do you exert on those that work for you?

Managing your Time Effectively

This checklist is for all managers who wish to manage their time more effectively.

Good time management has always been an important skill, but it is now essential. Factors such as widespread corporate restructuring, accelerating change, information overload and the need to balance private and working lives have put the squeeze on managers to get much more from their working day.

MCI Standards

This checklist has relevance for the MCI Management Standards: Key Role C – Manage People.

Definition

Time management is a vital aspect of self management. It involves utilising time to create maximum personal effectiveness and efficiency. This is achieved by planning how best to use your time and successfully implementing the plan.

Advantages

Effective time management enables you to:

- achieve control over your activities and increase the efficiency of your work
- achieve a good balance between work, rest and play
- become proactive rather than reactive in your management style
- deal with problems as they arise rather than letting them grow
- build in time for constructive personal development
- save money by increasing efficiency and achieving more
- complete important tasks on time and avoid wasting time on unimportant tasks
- have time to listen to others

- be well-perceived by others and differentiated from less well-organised colleagues
- relieve pressure and stress
- go home from the office on time.

Action checklist

1. Establish how your time is spent

Look back through your diary or logsheet to work out how you spend your time. If you have not done so, log your activities for a period of two weeks to see where your time is going. Ask yourself:

- how much of your activity was a result of planning and how much was unplanned
- how accurate your planning was – did you complete tasks in the time allowed?
- how much time was spent on routine activities which could be delegated
- how often interruptions diverted you from your tasks
- at what time of day you accomplished most.

2. Determine your problem areas

What is making you use time inefficiently? Split problems into the Enemy Without and the Enemy Within. The Enemy Without includes external factors beyond your immediate control, such as mistakes or inefficiencies of other departments, unexpected extra tasks, and complaints. The Enemy Within is personal inefficiency, and includes poor planning, lack of assertiveness in turning away unwanted callers, and putting off problems and unenjoyable activities.

3. Be clear on your objectives and priorities

Before you can successfully manage your time, you must make sure that you are familiar with your job description and with what you should and should not be doing as part of your job. Agree your precise role, objectives and targets with both your superiors and subordinates so that everyone knows what is expected of you, and put this in writing.

4. Tackle the Enemy Without

If you find that problem relationships, complaints, and reaction to situations beyond your control take up too much of your time, try to minimise this by:

- setting service level agreements which detail what each department expects from others, and improving interdepartmental communication
- reviewing complaints procedures and setting up a more efficient system

- examining personnel policies which might be giving rise to interpersonal tension or inefficient work practices
- asking colleagues to be concise when giving written or oral reports.

5. Tackle the Enemy Within

Make more constructive use of your time by:

Planning
- map out your activities a week in advance
- spend five minutes each morning reviewing your time
- plan and adjust it as circumstances change
- build slack time into your schedule so that you do not constantly overrun
- have a back-up plan for contingency situations – decide which tasks can be dropped, who can be called on to help out, and who will need to be notified if you are consequently delayed with other activities
- plan time for relaxation and recreation as well as work.

Prioritising
- rank tasks in order of importance – try to be objective and avoid ranking highly those tasks which you enjoy but are not that vital
- be firm but polite in refusing to do tasks which are not your responsibility
- maintain clear objectives on what you are trying to achieve and allocate your time accordingly.

Delegating
- assess which tasks can be delegated to someone else
- choose carefully who you delegate to – is the person knowledgeable and competent in this area? Does he or she have the time and willingness to do the task? Will you be offending anyone else?
- make sure you give clear instructions so that the task is done well
- give regular routine tasks to your secretary – fifteen minutes spent showing him or her how to do it will result in hours being saved over a year
- involve others in projects and share the workload
- train your employees to manage their time effectively too.

Reviewing how you work
- plan to do important activities at the time of day when you function best
- break down complex tasks into manageable chunks
- avert unwanted interruptions – if necessary, ask your secretary to ward off unwanted callers, work somewhere other than your office, or simply put a 'Do Not Disturb' sign on the door (make sure that people know it means what it says)
- work at home for a day occasionally, if this is allowed and if home is a quiet environment
- talk to people instead of writing – this can result in a quicker response and quicker decision making

- avoid task hopping – concentrate on one thing at a time
- batch similar tasks together
- have breaks or switch tasks when you feel tired or have a mental block
- keep accurate records and an organised filing system to save time locating information or having to compile documents again
- make use of new technology – but only if it really will save time
- minimise paperwork and avoid unnecessary duplication
- make sure the meetings you attend are really necessary and if running one yourself make sure it is well-organised
- look at your travel arrangements for commuting or work trips – can you eliminate unnecessary journeys or shorten them?

6. Make time to play

Overwork is counter-productive. It can cause stress and unhappiness, and decrease the time efficiency which you worked so hard to achieve. However well-organised you are, there are still only 24 hours in a day and you need to devote an adequate proportion of them to yourself. Don't be afraid to take ten minutes for a tea break or a walk around the park, or an hour to go to the gym. Try to maintain a healthy work / home-life balance.

Dos and don'ts for effective time management

Do
- Clarify your objectives and targets.
- Assess priorities and constantly review them as circumstances change.
- Be firm and assertive with unwanted time stealers.
- Make sure your time plan is efficient but realistic.

Don't
- Equate being busy with being efficient.
- Attempt to do more than you are capable of.
- Give priority to the loudest claim on your time – it may not be the most important.
- Assume your plans are rigid – environments and situations change and you will need to adapt.
- See time management as purely a work issue – it is a personal issue and spans both work and home and the balance between them.

Useful reading
First things first: how to manage your time for maximum performance, Patrick Forsyth, London: Pitman Publishing, 1994
Successful time management in a week, 2nd ed, Declan Treacy, London: Hodder & Stoughton, 1998
Time management, Martin Scott, London: Century Business, 1992
Right on time: the complete guide for pressured managers, Lester R Bittel, New York: McGraw Hill, 1991

Thought starters

- Do you feel in control of your day?
- Do you have a plan of what you intend to accomplish each day?
- Do you keep both a diary of appointments and a diary of what actually happened?
- Do you put off tasks which you don't like doing?
- Are you frustrated by interruptions and unnecessary demands on your time?
- Do you agree to do things that you know someone else should be doing?
- Are you kept waiting by other people? Do you keep others waiting?
- Is your social or family life suffering because of pressure at work and long hours?
- Do you get enough time to yourself?

Handling Information – Avoiding Overload

This checklist is for those who are concerned with the ever increasing amount of information they are required to handle and describes a structured approach to controlling information overload.

In a climate of uncertainty where it is difficult to spot a real opportunity from a red herring, there are twin problems in controlling the amount of information to a level that is manageable, and in extracting any gems from the mass available. Too much information causes anxiety, stress and inefficiency; insufficient information leads to ineffective decision making, management by guesswork, even stagnation and decline.

Controlling information flow requires a highly disciplined and consistent approach to the processes of selection and evaluation.

MCI Standards

This checklist has relevance for the MCI Management Standards: Key Role D – Manage Information.

Definition

For the purposes of this checklist, 'information' is used in its widest sense and includes both written and oral, formal and informal communication.

To effectively handle information overload, many management skills are required. These, along with the organisation and delivery of information are covered in checklists on Report Writing, Effective Business Writing and Managing Your Time Effectively contained within this book.

Action checklist

1. Know yourself

Get to grips with how much new or continuing information you can cope with at any one time – people differ a lot in their capacity to handle information. Establish how you deal with the various ways information presents itself – do you write notes of conversations or do you rely on memory?

Acknowledge that information may appear on demand (you look for it) or with serendipity (a colleague tells you something in passing), and that both are valid and important ways.

2. Manage your time

If information swamps you continuously, set aside an amount of time each day or week for information activities such as evaluation. Stick to the time limits you set. Think about:

- how much time is available for work?
- how flexible is this?
- how much time can be spent on information processing?

3. Focus on objectives

Focus on current objectives, otherwise the information you might accumulate under the umbrella of 'may be useful at some time in the future' could overwhelm you from the outset. It is important to define objectives and priorities – for information purposes – in terms of 'must have', 'nice to have' and 'not necessary for me to keep'. Concentrate on what you need to know, not on what might be nice to know. When time is pressured these objectives will contract; occasionally there will be time for them to expand.

MUSTs include those bits of information which:

- have defined objectives
- are task-oriented
- relate to needs
- fit a designated purpose
- help with knowledge and understanding to progress activities.

NICE to HAVEs include information which:

- might be useful one day
- is unsolicited and unnecessary.

NOT NECESSARYs are often obvious but also include information which:

- is easily obtainable on demand
- won't cause any damage if missed.

4. Choose access and delivery methods

Choosing access and delivery methods is important throughout any cycle of information control. The medium can influence the message, even drown it if we are not careful. All information sources consume time in different ways:

- libraries of printed materials for the selection, processing and organising of items discovered can take ages to sift and sort

- the ease of retrieval from databases or the Internet can leave you with hundreds of references which can be very time-consuming to narrow down for relevance
- Internet newsgroups which promise to provide all you need on a subject but finish up by flooding you with masses of unedited data
- a message, sent email for convenience, leaves you printing out 80 pages...

At least libraries are organised – be especially wary of the others. Choose your medium with care, otherwise you are more likely to end up with too much poor-quality information which will need culling. Keep objectives and selection criteria firmly in mind. Get to know sources of information and learn how to use them; you will then be able to retrieve most information when you need it.

5. Establish selection criteria

We either deal with information immediately it arrives because it is something which enables us to further our course of action, or we:

- pass it on to someone else – this may just be passing the problem on rather than solving it, unless you know that the recipient has a need for it
- save it for a rainy day – this means that you become weighed down with clutter which takes time to organise, and may not give a profitable return (not even the largest of electronic libraries can hold everything people might need)
- get rid of it – this is often the only sensible, practical option.

Asking the following questions should help determine which of these is the best course to follow.

- Do I need this NOW? Can I use it on a current project?
- Where does this come from? Is the source reliable, reputable?
- Did I ask for it? If it hadn't arrived, would I have gone looking for it?
- Is it speculative or substantiated? Is it controversial?
- Is it directly about the subject in question?
- Is it worth keeping for the future? Could I get hold of it if the need arose? Would I know where to go for it?
- Is it worth passing to someone else?
- Does it need a lot of re-working to make it intelligible?
- Should I keep a note of it and if so in what form?

A standard rule-of-thumb must be – don't keep useless information; quality information is everything.

6. Gain confidence in what you know

We do not know what we do not know. However, when we read new material in the hope of finding new ideas, we discover that we are aware of most of its contents and its reading has not added to the sum of our knowledge, although we do have the comfort reaction of feeling up-to-date.

It is important to gain a picture of how often this happens, and how often something striking and worthwhile comes your way. This might provide you with your own 80-20 rule. Allied to your knowledge of proven/best/reliable/innovative sources, this may begin to cut down on the quantities of repeat information heaped on you.

7. Consult

Often a face-to-face conversation is worth a thousand memos and reports – it is a question of investing initial time to make savings later. Your colleagues are probably your best source of information, but should be supplemented by your own short-list of experts you can trust to help you cut your way through to what you really need. This may include a professional body, special library, government department, TEC or Business Link. If you want to get to grips with a subject, get hold of a summary article, digest or checklist from a reputable source.

Most organisations have 'gate-keepers' – people who gather large quantities of information and are good communicators. These people can help you to sift and filter information. Find your own gate-keeper if you don't have one already.

8. Be ruthless with paperwork

- Remove your name selectively from external and internal mailing lists.
- Ask colleagues to report by exception, and then to be concise: 1-page management.
- Return unnecessary paperwork to sender, or bin it.
- Adopt a sanguine approach to computer labels addressed to a long-departed predecessor.
- If you can use someone else as a 'sifter', do so – but make sure they are not overloaded too.

9. Beware the information junkie

We have all come across them – the verbose who love the sound of their own voice, who cannot restrict themselves to short, concise thoughts or words of less than four syllables and who just waffle on for the sake of exploiting otherwise invaluable oxygen and persist in long rambling sentences which make you lose track of the argument....

Such junkies become lethal on a computer network; their persistent electronic questions and answers can eat into days of your time and jam up the whole system. There is a simple solution: a one-word answer or no answer at all.

10. Be ruthless with electronic data, especially on the Internet

- Work out personal screening procedures, for example, culling by source of origin.
- Exploit software which ranks information content for relevance rather than scan through hundreds of documents.
- Don't pass on messages which 'might' be of use; give them only to those who you know will be interested.
- Be wary of subscribing to too many open newsgroups, where all comments from everyone are circulated to everyone.
- Remember the delete key. With too much dross there is a swift, although final, answer.

Dos and don'ts for handling information and avoiding overload

Do

- Review priorities as circumstances change.
- Differentiate the need to, from the nice to, know.
- Focus on current objectives.
- Know your information sources.

Don't

- Become a slave to routine activities which have lost pertinence.
- Tolerate unsolicited dross.
- Deal with a piece of paper twice.

Useful reading

Managing information in a week, Bob Norton, London: Hodder & Stoughton, 1995

To know or not to know: the politics of information, Reuters Business Information, London: Reuters, 1994

Dying for information? An investigation into the effects of information overload in the UK and worldwide, Reuters Business Information, London: Reuters, 1996

Thought starters

- Does new paper go on top of old in the in-tray?
- Have you assessed the bottom-line value of the unsolicited information you receive?
- Are you clear on current information objectives?
- 'The New York Times contains as much distinctive information every day as the average 17th Century person encountered in a lifetime' (The Independent, 15 October 1996, p6).
- 'Knowledge is of two kinds. We know a subject ourselves, or we know where we can find information upon it' (Samuel Johnson).
- One in four managers suffers ill health because of the amount of information handled.

Successful Delegation

> **This checklist has been designed to explain how to succeed at delegation.**
>
> **Delegation is a vital management skill, but some managers don't delegate effectively, often out of fear of letting go. They hold the mistaken belief that nobody else can do the job as well as they can. Others feel they simply haven't got the time to delegate an activity and that it's easier to do the job themselves.**
>
> **The key is to make sure that you delegate, but don't abdicate on the one hand or interfere on the other.**

MCI Standards

This checklist has relevance for the MCI Management Standards: Key Role C – Manage People.

Definition

Delegation is about entrusting others with appropriate responsibility and authority for the operation and/or accomplishment of certain activities. More simply, it is about getting someone else to do part of your job – a job that is your responsibility but need not be done by yourself. It isn't getting them to do something they're already paid to do in the first place. It should also be positive (for instance as a means of developing staff) rather than negative (for example passing on a job you don't like).

There are various levels of delegation.

You may wish to delegate the activity but not the accountability. Because you're delegating part of your job, you remain ultimately responsible for the outcome. You get the credit if you delegate effectively, but you also get the criticism if your delegation is less than successful.

You may wish to delegate responsibility and authority for the activity, leaving the delegate to get on with it. This is where it is important not to abdicate, and to maintain a fine balance between interest, support and motivation on the one hand, and interference or neglect on the other.

Advantages of delegation

Effective delegation:

- frees up time for managers
- helps managers prioritise their work
- helps managers assess the potential of their people
- is highly motivating for the people to whom work is delegated – they get to do more challenging work
- acts as a development tool by increasing the range of skills in a team
- helps with succession planning by exposing people to other levels of work.

Issues involved in delegation

There are no real disadvantages to delegation but there are some issues to consider:

- Delegation takes time and managers need to put considerable effort and personal investment into it.
- There is a level of risk – people take on part of the job but effectively the buck stops with you.
- Because of the recent spate of downsizing in organisations, you may simply not have people with sufficient resources, time or competence to delegate to.

Action checklist

1. Be consistent

Ask yourself if the particular activity to be delegated is a one-off, or part of a general trend or framework of assigning activities to others and of developing their skills. It is important to be consistent so that staff understand what to expect and a climate of trust starts to build.

It is important to work out – with your boss as well as with those for whom you are responsible – the boundaries of responsibility which enable your people to:

- take a decision on their own with no need to report to you
- take a decision and then report to you
- take a decision only after discussion with you.

Vagueness about boundaries of responsibility is common and is the cause of much confusion in organisations.

2. Identify the activity to be delegated

Be clear on what you want to delegate. Ask yourself what end result you want (in terms of people development as well as activity) and use this as the basis for deciding what to delegate.

Delegate whole activities rather than parts. If you delegate the whole activity, it raises the satisfaction level of the person carrying it out, develops them, and also helps them to really understand the job.

3. Think through the benefits of delegation

Clarify with yourself exactly what the benefits are of delegation. Firstly think through how it will benefit:

- you
- the person to whom you're delegating the activity
- the team
- the department
- the organisation
- the customers.

Only when you're clear about the benefits to most or some of them will you be able to sell the idea that it is worth the individual taking on the delegated activity. The act of explaining the activity is one of the key ways of gaining commitment to it, so you need to be clear about the benefits even at this early stage.

On the other hand, try to assess possible problems:

- What might happen if things don't work out?
- What is the worst case scenario for the team, the organisation, or the customers?
- What negative impact might this have on the individual?
- How much support should you give?

4. Identify the person

Make sure you are not too one-dimensional when selecting the right person for the job. It is all too easy to choose someone you've chosen before. Start afresh with a clean piece of paper and really work through what the job is, and the skills and attributes required. Ask yourself whether you want someone, for example:

- who is reliable, with plenty of experience
- who will take a risk but bring about a quick result
- whose development will benefit from the challenge
- who will simply absorb the workload as a matter of routine.

5. Negotiate the delegated activity

Delegation works best when the person taking on the activity fully understands what is required of them, and is enthusiastic and willing to do it.

This process may need to be carried out in quite minute detail. If you're delegating the writing of a report, you may need to specify the way the information should be presented, the arguments or hypotheses you need exposed, and even the number of pages it should contain.

Sit down with the individual and come to an agreement with them about what they're going to do, when they're going to do it, what resources they will need and the outcome that is expected.

Sell the benefits to the person. Explain exactly what's in it for them and check they're happy doing it. Do elicit, or listen to, the delegate's thoughts or fears and allow for them as you clarify and agree goals. Remember, they do have the right to say no, and if they do, you must try not to hold this against them.

6. Allocate time and be supportive

Allocate the right amount of time. Agree a schedule and arrange to meet up and compare notes. After a few weeks, check how the activity is going.

Remember you aren't simply just dumping work on them – you're actually working with them to make sure they can carry out the work you want. You should make sure you're available to them so that they can come and talk to you if they have a problem or need advice.

7. Work out the right level of responsibility with authority

If you are delegating a part of your job which needs authority, make sure that the delegate knows they have your full support, and that other people in the organisation are aware of this too. If the delegated activity involves other sections, make sure that the appropriate people understand what is happening, why and with whose authority.

8. Make it happen

The routes by which delegates achieve what is required are up to them.

Do not specify how the job actually has to be done. Remember you've just delegated an activity – it is up to the person concerned to come up with the best way of making sure that it happens. Allow the person to get on with the delegated activity and complete it. Once you have provided the resources they need to do the job, make sure you don't interfere but are there to support them.

9. Review and evaluate

When they have completed the activity, carry out a review to see how well it went. Evaluate the positive outcomes in terms of the activity and the skills or learning which have accrued. Be constructive on any failures and try to establish what could be done better next time for yourself as much as for the delegate.

Dos and don'ts for successful delegation

Do

- Plan the delegation properly.
- Negotiate with the person concerned. Be specific about the outcomes.
- Let go, and allow them to complete the job effectively.

Don't

- Leave people to sink or swim.
- Interfere or dictate how the job should be done.
- Delegate to the same people all the time.
- Take all the credit.

Useful reading

Empowering employees through delegation, Robert B Nelson, Burr Ridge, Ill: Irwin, 1994

Letting go without losing control: how to delegate and do more, John Payne and Shirley Payne, London: Pitman, 1994

Delegating for results, Robert B Maddux, London: Kogan Page, 1990

Delegation, Andrew Forrest, London: Industrial Society Press, 1989

Don't do, delegate: the secret power of successful managers, James M Jenks and John M Kelly, London: Kogan Page, 1985

Thought starters

- Have you ever been guilty of dumping work on someone else and wondering why it went wrong?
- Have you failed to provide the resources needed to help the person carry out the activity properly?
- Have you left enough time to make sure they can do it well?
- Have you delegated the authority to do the job properly?

Handling Effective Meetings

This checklist is for all involved in planning and chairing meetings.

MCI Standards

This Checklist has relevance for the MCI Management Standards: Key Role D – Manage Information.

Definition

For this checklist, a 'meeting' is defined as a group of three or more individuals arranged for a specific time, place and purpose. It does not cover meetings between two individuals, or purely accidental encounters, important as both these events may be!

Advantages of meetings

Meetings may not always be necessary or efficient. It is important to ensure that they are justified before committing the time, effort and other costs involved.

In the right situation, effective meetings can:

- provide swift and effective communication between a number of people
- be an effective decision making instrument
- enhance the motivation and commitment of a team.

Disadvantages of meetings

Some of the least effective meetings are those that are held regularly, such as every week or every month. Whether regular or not, ineffective or unnecessary meetings can:

- waste time and money
- exacerbate divisions and bad feeling
- produce poor decisions.

Action checklist

To be fully effective, appropriate action will be necessary before, at and after a meeting. Responsibility for success rests not only on the organiser and Chair, but on all participants.

Before the meeting

1. Ask 'Do I really need a meeting?' Consider what the purpose of the meeting is: to exchange information; to monitor progress on performance; to deal with specific problems; to brainstorm an issue; or to develop future plans. Only when you have done so can you decide the best timing, attendance and format of the meeting.

2. Set clear, precise objectives (not the agenda) for the meeting.

3. Decide who should be present; neither too many nor too few.

4. Choose the date, starting and finishing time, and place. Few meetings need to last longer than two hours at most.

5. Set the agenda. For each item clarify the objective and who will lead the discussion. Construct a timetable so that important items do not get squeezed out and lesser items do not absorb disproportionate time.

6. Make administrative arrangements, including:

   ● choose and book a suitable room
   ● ensure necessary equipment and supplies will be available
   ● arrange catering.

7. Notify all involved as early as possible. The notification should include:

   ● full details of date, time and place
   ● list of invitees
   ● the agenda
   ● reports and other supporting papers.

8. Arrange for secretarial help at the meeting.

9. Complete personal research, reading and other preparation.

10. Consider meeting objectives and strategy.

11. Consider whether to make appropriate advance contact with any participants whose contributions may be critical to the success of the meeting.

At the meeting the Chair/leader should

1. Arrive in good time.

2. Check that all arrangements, including equipment, seating and refreshments, are in order.

3. Welcome participants on arrival (especially newcomers).

4. Undertake any pre-meeting contacts necessary with key participants, but do not appear to fix things beforehand.

5. Start promptly.

6. Deal with administrative items:

   - introductions of newcomers, congratulations, thanks, good wishes, condolences, apologies etc
   - message-taking, car parking, smoking, catering etc
   - timing of breaks, end of meeting.

7. Despatch routine items.

8. Introduce each agenda item effectively, with emphasis on the objectives.

9. Shape and control the discussion:

   - encourage the shy
   - restrain the verbose and opinionated
   - allow only one discussion at a time
   - separate different subjects
   - 'hold' on subjects that are not exhausted
   - balance contributions on contentious subjects
   - keep control of time
   - use visual aids where they can help to make your point
   - don't express an opinion unless needed at the end
   - summarise at intervals
   - seek clear decisions at the appropriate point
   - express appreciation for members' contributions.

10. Conclude firmly and tidily, emphasising action points agreed.

11. Keep creative and analytical discussion separate. Creative meetings need a more relaxed timetable and atmosphere. It is hard to switch from the routine to the creative and vice versa.

After the meeting

1. Write down immediately the decisions taken, the actions agreed with the persons responsible for action and the dates by which action should be achieved.

2. Distribute the note to all participants and to others whom it may concern.

3. Monitor the progress of subsequent action.

Dos and don'ts for effective meetings

Do

- Consider other ways in which the objectives of a proposed meeting can be achieved.
- Prepare thoroughly – well in advance.
- Arrive in good time.
- Consider participants' comfort and convenience (eg smoking, ventilation, acoustics and noise levels, breaks etc).
- Use visual aids where useful.
- Focus on the objectives for each item.
- Ensure all contribute what they can to the discussion.
- Maintain good but not oppressive discipline.
- Aim for consensus whenever possible.

Don't

- Take notes if you are also the leader or a key contributor.
- Lose your temper.
- Get involved in purely personal disagreements.
- Talk too much or for too long.
- Insist on having the last word.
- Talk first, except to introduce a topic.
- Let the meeting run on and on.

How to assess meeting effectiveness

As with other activities, assessment of effectiveness will depend on having set clear objectives in advance, for the whole meeting and for individual items. Common measures of effectiveness include:

- Did all present contribute positively, according to their roles?
- Was the discussion lively but good-tempered throughout?
- Were all relevant aspects of the subjects properly explored?
- Was consensus reached on all major decisions?
- Did the meeting cover the subjects within the time allotted?
- Did all leave with clear knowledge of what had been achieved, and their own responsibilities for future action?
- Ask participants to complete a brief evaluation; they perceive their own weaknesses and do better next time.

Evaluation form

To what extent ...	Poor				Good
Were the objectives clear?	1	2	3	4	5
Was it well-prepared?	1	2	3	4	5
Did it stick to the point?	1	2	3	4	5
Were vital matters covered?	1	2	3	4	5
Were clear decisions made?	1	2	3	4	5
Was people's knowledge used?	1	2	3	4	5
Did people speak freely?	1	2	3	4	5
Did you feel involved?	1	2	3	4	5
Did you contribute?	1	2	3	4	5
Did the Chair control the meeting?	1	2	3	4	5

Useful reading

Books

Successful meetings in a week, John Payne and Shirley Payne, London: Hodder & Stoughton, 1994

Let's have a meeting, Leslie Rae, London: McGraw Hill, 1994

How to make meetings work, Malcolm Peel, London: Kogan Page, 1990

Thought starters

- Was the last meeting you called/attended really necessary?
- Do you always prepare for meetings, whether as Chair or participant, thoroughly and in advance?
- Who is the best meeting leader you have worked with? Why was he/she so effective?
- Who is the worst meeting leader you have worked with? Why was he/she so ineffective?

Brainstorming

> **The purpose of this checklist is to enable a busy manager, without previous experience of the technique and with a minimum of preparation, to introduce brainstorming to a group and then go on to brainstorm a specific problem or opportunity.**

MCI Standards

This checklist has relevance for the MCI Management Standards: Key Role D – Manage Information.

Definition

Brainstorming involves a spontaneous, open-ended discussion in a search for new ideas. It is a means of getting a large number of ideas from a group of people in a short time. It can prove valuable for identifying opportunities, for example, for market development, tackling organisational problems or problem solving in general.

Advantages

- Numerous fresh ideas and concepts are rapidly generated.
- It enables people to be involved and make a positive contribution.
- The cost of the process – in terms of people and time – is quantifiable.

Problems

- The session can be dictated or sidetracked by dominant individuals.
- Getting people to be non-critical can be a problem.

These problems can be overcome by a good facilitator. See step 3 below.

Action checklist – Preparation

1. Select the problem / opportunity to be brainstormed

Select an item important enough to justify the participation of others. It should also be one where there are a number of possible solutions and imagination is required to think of them.

2. Think of structure, aims and objectives

Although a brainstorming session is an open, 'no-holds-barred' affair, establish where you are going, what you want to achieve and roughly how to get there.

3. Choose the facilitator …

… an open, outgoing person with enthusiasm and ability, contributing interest and enjoyment. Choosing the right facilitator is vital. S/he need not be the most senior person at the session, but will need to set the scene by relaxing the participants and creating an open, free atmosphere, controlling dominant people, getting and keeping them on track by highlighting the issues, and creating a sense of fun. Perhaps most importantly, s/he should be adept at keeping ideas flowing.

Should the facilitator be internal or external? An external facilitator can be especially useful when senior managers are involved, but if the issue is not too complex or contentious, an internal facilitator may be used provided s/he has some experience.

The facilitator should feel comfortable running activity-based sessions, and should have clear plans and tactics for arriving at expected outcomes or targets. The facilitator must also ensure, as much as possible, that the group works as a team and owns what it has achieved at the end.

4. Select an appropriate venue

This depends largely on the time set aside for the session. If time is available then somewhere away from the routine place of work is often more suitable. This gets people away from 'contemplating their corporate navel' and is often better for a fresh perspective on the business in hand.

5. Think of the group mix

As well as those with a specialist contribution to make include those who have little or no knowledge of the problem to be brainstormed. They will not be concerned with detail and will offer a fresh approach. Consider the introduction of outsiders for this, although it can backfire if they are seen as intruders or spies. Work on getting the group dynamics right for putting the group at ease, avoidance of snide or put-down comments and creating a 'free-from-blame' atmosphere. All participants are equal and none are more equal than others.

6. Think of the right number

There is no right number, although more than 10 might be unmanageable when ideas really start to flow, and less than five might not be enough for generating creativity. Six to eight is usually about right, although this will depend on the style of the facilitator and the nature of the problem to be tackled.

7. Get the equipment right

You will need to record the ideas that come up. A tape-recorder smacks of 'big brother' and may well act as an inhibitor to the free flow of ideas. Get hold of a flip-chart – with plenty of sheets and plenty of marker pens that work! – so that successive sheets can be blu-tacked to the wall in full view and therefore help to stimulate further ideas.

8. Get the layout right

Do not use a room with fixed rows of seats. Something more relaxed, even random, is preferable; a circle or U-shape is fairly usual. If the facilitator is not familiar with the room to be used, s/he should check it beforehand and prepare it appropriately.

9. Get the timing right

Think of your own powers of concentration and remember that brainstorming of ideas can go from dynamic to exhausted, and back again. 10-20 minutes may be needed to get people relaxed; two hours can be a long time to brainstorm – stop for a break if people show signs of tiredness. Arrange for a 20-minute break after an hour's uninterrupted flow, or if and when the flow slows to a trickle. The break may be enough to stimulate an active re-start, perhaps with a change in seating of individuals.

10. Get the time of day right

Unfortunately hard advice is difficult here as we are all different. Some people are better when their mind is less active and more relaxed and when their routine work has been dispensed with. Others may prefer the morning when collective mental energy is at its highest, or at least not dulled by the day's toil.

Provide sufficient notice of the session, and an outline of the problem to be tackled.

Action checklist – The session

1. State the problem/objective

State the problem and explain it to the group. Make sure everyone participating has a clear understanding.

2. Restate the problem

Encourage the group to stand back from the problem, walk around it, and see it from every angle. Suggest re-wording it in 'How to..' statements. Some restatements may be close to the original, others may illuminate new facets. Jot down the restatements on the flip-chart for all to see.

3. Brainstorm the problem with the following guidelines:

a) Suspend judgement: avoid evaluative comments such as 'that won't work' or 'that sounds silly'. Laugh with wild ideas, not at them.

b) Use the following techniques for generating further ideas.

- Call for a one-minute break, asking the group to look over ideas already noted before starting the flow again.
- Offer a target: eg 'we just need six more to make 50 ideas!'
- Reflect and concentrate on one idea, eg how many ways can we do this?
- Look back at the re-statements to pursue other lines.

c) Freewheel: encourage (within limits) drifting or dreaming; try to bring the subconscious into play; the wilder the idea, the better.

d) Go for quantity not quality – the more the merrier; suspend judgement, evaluation comes later.

e) Cross-fertilise: pick up somebody's idea and suggest others leading from it.

4. Ask the group to choose a really wild and apparently senseless idea from the lists marked up and generate ideas from there

5. Closure

Give a warning of when the session will close five minutes from the end. The participants will want to know what happens next. Explain that the lists will be typed up for circulation. Do this within 24 hours to retain freshness and familiarity. Tell the participants that they will be informed on the ideas chosen for further action or recommendation. Ask them one last time for any comments, ideas or further thinking. Evaluation does not matter at this stage as the ideas will already be gathered; evaluation comes next.

Action checklist – Evaluation

1. Get the team to scrutinise all the ideas to pick out any instant winners

Use a process of ranking with 3 points for those which stand out, 2 points for those which have possibilities but need a little adjustment, and zero for those which now appear over the top, require clearly too much resource, or do not meet the orginal objectives.

2. Reduce the number of '2s' to a minimum by applying such criteria as cost, acceptability or time-scales

3. Use reverse brainstorming

- In how many ways can a particular idea fail?
- What are the negative factors?
- What is the potential downside for the organisation?

4. Apply the key evaluative criteria

- What will it cost?
- Will it be acceptable to management, staff, customers?
- Is it legal?
- Is it practical?
- How long will it take?
- What competition will there be?
- How urgent is it? (If it is not done now, will an opportunity be lost?)

Dos and don'ts for brainstorming

Do

In the brainstorming session, the facilitator should:

- be sensitive to participants' tiredness
- encourage freedom of movement – some people think better when mobile
- use a variety of techniques to generate further ideas
- encourage an informal atmosphere free from blame or inhibition.

Don't

S/he should not:

- let the session go on too long
- allow interruptions
- use a tape-recorder
- allow critical or evaluative comments
- allow the session to become too 'off-the-wall'!

Useful reading

Constructive brainstorming can jump the gaps, Tony Buzan, Business Marketing Digest, Vol 18(1), 1993, pp35–41

Brainstorm with a stranger, Garrod Whatley, Chief Executive, March 1987, pp36–37

Brainstorming electronically, R Brent Gallupe and William H Cooper, Sloan Management Review, Vol 35(1), 1993, pp27–36

Creativity at work, Tudor Rickards, Aldershot: Gower, 1988

Successful problem solving: the organised approach to creative solutions, Dean Francis Juniper, London: Foulsham, 1989

Thought starters

Does your organisation need to:

- become more innovative?
- solve problems requiring creative or imaginative answers?
- get more involvement and participation from colleagues?
- generate ideas rapidly?

Solving Problems

This checklist outlines the systematic method of problem solving first put forward by Kepner and Tregoe in their work The New Rational Manager.

With straightforward, common problems – for example, slugs eating the bedding plants – it is common sense to try a series of quick and tested solutions starting with the most simple or cheapest (slug-pellets) and then moving on to those which take longer to apply (changing the plants or soil). With problems of greater complexity it may not be so easy, or indeed advisable, to try quick solutions. The answer may lie in any one of a number of directions and the quick fix may do more harm than good. The Kepner-Tregoe method enables far more complex problems to be tackled, such as why staff morale is low, why sales are down, why complaints are up, or why industrial relations are worsening.

MCI Standards

This checklist has relevance for the MCI Management Standards: Key Role D – Manage Information.

Definition

Kepner and Tregoe define a problem as a deviation from the norm.

Problem solving differs fundamentally from decision making. A problem occurs when something is not behaving as it should; something is deviating from the norm; something goes wrong. Decision making is a case of choosing between different alternatives. Decision making is required for the question: 'Which computer shall I buy?'. Problem solving is needed for the statement: 'My computer won't work'.

Other approaches to problem solving can be tackled using Further Reading as a starting point.

Advantages

The process:

- is systematic and thorough
- provides evidence to show how the problem was solved
- helps avoid the rush to jump to a solution without knowing the cause of the problem
- enables possible causes to be tested
- is particularly suitable for complex or fuzzy problems.

Disadvantages

The process:

- is time-consuming and reliant on thorough investigation
- requires disciplined information-seeking and collation.

Action checklist

1. Define the problem

Investigate exactly what has gone wrong; do not be influenced by people with ready-made solutions. Try to identify the problem through signals from routine statistical returns, progress meetings, suggestion schemes, reports and letters. A rising tide of complaints, for example, could stem from faulty machinery, poor packaging, staff absence, poor staff training, product deficiency, false marketing hype and so on. Getting the definition accurate is crucial; otherwise you might find that you are solving the wrong problem and collecting possible answers to questions that have not been asked.

2. Gather relevant information

This is a key step, involving all factors which may have an influence on the problem. Go into detail on the people, activities, processes, equipment, systems, time-scales and conditions under which the problem occurs.

Ask the following:

- What is the problem?   eg Productivity on the shop-floor.
  What is not the problem?   eg Equipment, working conditions.
  What is different about the problem? eg The time it started.

- Who is affected by it?   eg Staff on shop-floor.
  Who is not affected by it?   eg Clerical, administrative staff.
  What is different about those   eg A continuing rise in
  affected?   absenteeism.

- What things are affected by   eg Meeting production targets,
  the problem?   deadlines, quality requirements.
  What things are not affected?   eg Machine capacity, skill
     requirements.

  What is distinctive about   eg Rumblings of discontent; lack
  those affected?   of cooperation.

3. Identify possible causes

Causes usually relate to people, systems or equipment. Be careful not to
blame the tool when it could be the operator. The question – what has
changed from the norm – helps to identify the cause.

- When did the problem first occur?   eg 6-7 weeks ago.
  When did it not exist?   eg Before then.
  What changed?   eg The introduction of new work
     teams.

- What changes might be relevant?   eg New work practices.

4. Identify a possible solution

Once you have identified a likely cause, work out an hypothesis to test
exactly what it is you are looking for and how you will know if you are
right. The cause of a problem is always a change from the norm that has
produced effects in some places but not in others. Find out where the effects
are not happening.

- What changes might be relevant?   New work practices.
- What causes might this suggest?   Imposition of new scheme?
     Lack of consultation?
     Inadequate training?
     Dominance of certain individuals?
     Implementation too rushed?

5. Test the possible causes

Go back over the information you have assembled in steps 1–4 to test, on
paper, if the cause finds a good match with how, where and when the problem occurs, to what extent it occurs, and who is affected by it.

6. Work out the solution

There may be a number of possible solutions (which may not be mutually exclusive), with some more appropriate than others. This is the time to move from problem analysis to a method for decision-making.

7. Make the decision

Identify alternative solutions and assess the consequences of implementing each. Testing solutions against causes provides one mechanism for doing this, group brainstorming (see the checklist on Brainstorming on p. 81) another. Select the most promising alternative and produce a plan showing a schedule of actions to be performed by whom, when.

There may not be an ideal solution, but there should be a 'best' one (even if best means 'least worst').

8. Monitor the results

Track the changes which occur because of what has been implemented. Take care to monitor how other changes might impact on the action you have chosen, and vice-versa.

Useful reading

The new rational manager, Charles H Kepner and Benjamin B Tregoe, London: John Martin, 1981
How to be a better problem solver, Michael Stevens, London: Kogan Page, 1996
Solve that problem: a practical guide to solving business problems, Geoff Cox, London: Pitman, 1995
Problem solving for results, Victor Newman, Aldershot: Gower, 1995
Effective problem solving, Martin Levine, 2nd ed, Englewood Cliffs, NJ: Prentice Hall, 1994
Problem solving techniques that really work, Malcolm Bird, London: Piatkus, 1992

Dos and don'ts for problem solving

Do
- Keep asking the key questions: what, when, where and who?
- Gather as much relevant information as possible.
- Define the exact nature of the problem.
- Keep a record of the information you collate for re-checking.

Don't
- Forget the key principle of opposites, or negatives: what not? when not? where not? who not?
- Neglect to test possible causes against the data gathered.
- Jump to an apparently obvious solution without evidence.
- Evaluate ideas too quickly.

Thought starters

- When you have a problem, do you go for a choice, or a cause?
- Do you come across complex, fuzzy problems?
- Do you have a systematic approach to tackling problems?
- Do you rely on flashes of inspiration?

Managing Projects

This checklist outlines the steps in project management and provides a framework of sequential action for the manager undertaking a project.

Project management is recognised as a special process which differs in approach from general management or change management. The traditional project management focus has been that of completing defined work within given time constraints and cost limits. Recently the focus has shifted more to the quality of the final output delivered to the customer.

MCI Standards

This checklist has relevance for the MCI Management Standards: Key Role G – Manage Projects.

Definition

'Project management is a specialised management technique to plan and control projects ... A project is generally deemed successful if it meets pre-determined targets set by the client, performs the job it was intended to do, or solves an identified problem within the pre-determined time, costs and quality constraints.' – Burke.

Benefits of project management

Project management techniques provide:

- an appropriate way to bring about sudden, revolutionary or purposive change
- a suitable approach for handling one-off tasks
- a realistic method for evaluating a new scheme.

Problems with project management

Projects:

- often require an extraordinary use of resources – especially money and people – over a finite period of time
- usually consume more resources than foreseen
- can go over schedule by significant margins.

Action checklist

1. Define the objectives

Fundamental to the management of any successful project are both under-standing and agreement of:

- what is required to be achieved
- what is to be the outcome and/or delivered as a result
- dates and budgets for project completion by both project sponsor and project manager.

Lack of clear objectives will doom the project from the beginning.

2. Appoint the project manager

The project manager must be someone who has a proven track record, can command respect from a mix of seniorities and can get action from them. They should be able to:

- plan and communicate all aspects of the project
- motivate with integrity, sensitivity and imagination
- gain productivity and trust from shared decision-making
- lead both by example and by taking a back seat when appropriate
- monitor costs, efficiency and quality without excessive bureaucracy
- get things done right first time without being a slave-driver
- get the right people for the right task at the right time
- use both technical and general management skills to control the project
- see clear-sightedly through tangled issues.

3. Establish the terms of reference

The terms of reference specify the objectives, scope, time-frames and initial scale of resource required. They should also clarify any risks, constraints or assumptions already identified. It is important to make any early allowances for cost escalation, plans veering off course, and build in a level of contingency, or safety margin.

4. Construct the work breakdown structure document (WBSD)

Having established what the project should achieve, next consider how to achieve it.

The WBSD forms the basis of much subsequent work in planning, setting budgets, exercising control and assigning responsibilities. The key is to break the project down into identifiable phases, then into controllable units for action. Dividing a piece of work into more approachable, discrete units facilitates the functions of estimating, planning and controlling. As soon as possible allocate time-scales to each unit of work, taking care to allow for both sequential units – those that need to be accomplished before the next can be tackled, and overlapping units – those that can run in tandem.

5. Plan for quality

Planning for quality requires both attention to detail and ensuring that the project output or outcome does what it is supposed to, or is 'fit for its purpose'. The work breakdown structure should incorporate 'micro' performance criteria or indicators, for discrete units or phases, and 'macro' indicators against which the final outcome can be assessed. Quality measures (systematic inspections against established standards) should be built into the process from the beginning, not later when things (may) have started to go awry. The formula:

establish standards $\longrightarrow$ monitor performance $\longrightarrow$ take corrective action

can run as a continuous sequence throughout the project duration. The key is to ensure effective quality assurance which acts as a prevention rather than a cure and enables you to get things right first time.

6. Plan costs

A key area in which the most frequent error is to under-estimate costs. Typical cost elements include:

- staff time and wages – usually the most substantial cost item of all
- overheads – employer on-costs
- materials and supplies – the raw materials
- equipment – the pros and cons of leasing or purchasing and the factor of depreciation
- administration – purchasing, accounting, record-keeping.

One of the enabling functions of a good budget is to monitor costs while a project is in progress.

7. Plan time-scales

In order to calculate the shortest time necessary to complete the project you need to know:

- the earliest time a stage or unit can start
- the duration of each stage
- the latest time by which a stage must be completed.

Gantt charts, PERT diagrams and Critical Path Analysis are prominent amongst several project management techniques which can help with effective planning of time-scales.

8. Monitor and report progress

The monitoring of in-progress costs, time-scales and quality is a major factor for consideration throughout the duration of the project. Quality is the hardest to measure and, as such, prone to neglect.

In addition to progress reports, feedback sessions and Management By Walking About, there are various control tools which help check that implementation is going according to plan.

- Control Point Charts ask you what is likely to go wrong in terms of time, cost and quality.
- Project Control Charts provide status reports of actual costs against budget with variances.
- Milestone Charts are a means of showing stages of achievement as steps towards the project objectives.

It is important to know what to do when these, or other, control mechanisms indicate that something is going wrong. Contingency plans are also vital, as goalposts are always prone to movement.

9. Deliver the output

Haynes writes that 'the goal of project management is to obtain client acceptance of the project result'. Steps before delivery of the project outcome may include the compilation of instructional documentation or training packages. The penultimate stage before project completion is ensuring that the outcome of the project is accepted by the customer or sponsor.

10. Evaluate the project

By building in a final stage of evaluation it is possible to gain a measure of the project's success and see what lessons can be learned. Once again, the three key areas for review are quality, time and costs. Others include:

- staff skills gained or identified
- mistakes not to be repeated
- tools and techniques that were valuable
- what would be tackled differently.

Further reading

Successful project management in a week, 2nd ed, Mark Brown, London: Hodder & Stoughton, 1998

Project management, 6th ed, Dennis Lock, Aldershot: Gower, 1996

Project management: strategic design and implementation, 2nd ed, David I Cleland, New York: McGraw Hill, 1994

Project management planning and control, 2nd ed, Rory Burke, Chichester: John Wiley, 1993

Handbook of project-based management: improving the processes for achieving strategic objects, J Rodney Turner, Maidenhead: McGraw Hill, 1992

Some project management software suppliers

Arena Software Ltd, Cambridge, Tel: 01223 464194

Goldcrest Computer Services Ltd, Milton Keynes, Tel: 01908 211330

Microsoft Ltd, Reading, Tel. 0345 002000

PSDI (UK) Ltd, Woking, Tel: 01483 727000

Dos and don'ts of project management

Do

- Take time at the beginning on objectives, terms of reference and the work breakdown structure.
- Ensure, as far as possible, access to resources needed.
- Appoint someone with the right skill-mix as project manager.

Don't

- Let small changes creep in without assessing the implications.
- Omit to build in quality checks.
- Lose sight of time targets and budget limits.

Thought starters

Think of a job or task you have to do.

- Does it have a set start and finish date?
- Does it require a budget?
- Does it need other resources: people, equipment, raw materials?
- Does it involve changing something?
- Does it have a clear objective or target?

Effective Business Writing

This checklist is an introduction to the basic principles of business writing, which can take many forms. What is common to each of these forms is the importance of conveying the right message to the right audience in the right way – and at the right time. The effectiveness of business writing is measured not by whether the recipient enjoyed reading the communication, but by whether it achieved its purpose.

In an age when business communications are increasingly written in electronic form it is just as important for ideas and information to be conveyed clearly and concisely. Technology does not remove the need to write well.

MCI Standards

This checklist has relevance for the MCI Management Standards: Key Role D – Manage Information.

Definition

The term 'business writing' is used to cover any form of written communication within the context of paid employment, including letters, memos, public relations or marketing material, and a range of reports. (Report writing is the subject of a related checklist and is therefore mentioned only in passing here). Although different organisations may have their own styles, the same principles apply whether the writer is in the public or private sector, in a small business or in a large government department.

Action checklist

1. Decide what you are trying to achieve by writing

What is your main aim? How does this relate to the broader context of the organisation and the possibly conflicting aims of other people within it? Unless you think about this you will have no reference point by which to judge whether the communication is effective. Relate your objectives to the wider organisational picture.

2. Determine the action you want to happen as a result

What do you want to happen as a result of your communication? This will be closely linked to its purpose. If you want to impart facts, how will you know you have been successful? Be explicit about the action you expect recipients to take.

3. Check that a written communication is the most appropriate medium

Before you begin writing, decide and plan your message and then choose the right communication strategy. Only write if:

- you need to address a number of people
- the argument or explanation is complex or needs visual support
- you need a considered response
- you need an accurate and permanent record of the communication.

If the message is urgent, one to one, or can be expressed simply and without visual aid, consider phoning. Alternatively, if you need to involve several people in an urgent decision, or if action is conditional on presenting an argument to several people, seek a meeting first.

4. Consider who should 'sign off' the communication

The assumption is that you are writing the communication. However, its effectiveness may depend on it being seen to come from someone else. Its message may be more powerful if it is signed by someone more senior – or more junior. The important point is that the signature is of someone with the right credentials for the target readers.

5. Determine the right target audience

Ensure that the prospective audience is the right one to deliver the action you need – and that they are motivated to deliver it. Do they represent the right constituencies within the organisation? Will they have the authority to act?

6. Build a rapport with your audience

Getting readers to deliver what you need, even if it is only their attention, depends on building a rapport with them through setting the right tone. Three basic choices of tone are available:

- plead for the audience to do something on your behalf
- persuade them to do something by selling its benefits
- appeal to broader organisational interests and invoke the value of team work.

The last will usually be the most effective approach: try to establish common ground and express the issue in terms of its effect both on you and on the recipient.

7. Build a convincing argument

Develop a proposition that is compelling by spelling out the benefits and by anticipating and forestalling objections. See the issue from the recipient's perspective, understand their likely concerns and show how the proposal both addresses these and fits with overall organisational strategy. Be realistic about problems and the effort required to overcome them.

8. Prepare an outline

Note down the key strands of your argument in a few words and build a structure around them. Group key relationships and themes. The structure can be logical (a discussion of the issue, followed by evidence and conclusions) or declarative (the conclusion first, backed up by evidence).

9. Guide the reader around your text

Use the outline to begin writing. Whatever the structure or formality of the document, use clear signposts and flags to catch the reader's eye and guide them around. Provide an introduction which explains why you are writing and a summary which captures your key points. Separate out your conclusions and recommendations.

10. Make your text easy to read and unambiguous

Think about readability. Use short paragraphs and short sentences and avoid long or unfamiliar words. Use simple, direct expressions. Avoid jargon where possible; where it is unavoidable, explain it. Spell out abbreviations the first time you use them, even if you think your reader will be familiar with them. Use tangible rather than abstract concepts and use the active rather than passive voice ('he decided' rather than 'it was decided'), except where it is irrelevant or inappropriate to say who was responsible for the action. Use an occasional image to illustrate a point, but avoid language that is too flowery or informal. Only use humour occasionally and in good taste. Be grammatical – grammatical lapses and misspellings irritate readers and hinder their ability to receive messages.

11. Enliven your text with graphics

Use graphics to back up your arguments and convey your key messages – but only if they are clear and easy to read. Tell your audience when to look at them (by notes in the text) and where to find them. Include them in the main body of the text, with the exception of detailed statistical tables: these should be placed in an appendix at the back. Don't be tempted to use statistical tricks to bolster a weak argument: for example, distorting the 'y' axis of a graph to paint an overly favourable picture of a sales increase. The size of a graphic should relate to the importance of the point you are trying to make.

12. Revise your text once it is complete

Your communication will be effective only if it is authoritative. Read over your draft and be self-critical, or if you have time, ask someone you respect to read the text. Check that your reasoning and arguments form a logical sequence; ensure all your facts are right; give the source and authority for any opinions you cite; give due weight to contradictory arguments; and cover alternative conclusions or recommendations without being too dismissive of them. Be succinct: cast out any unnecessary bits and simplify the language if necessary.

13. Check the presentation of the text

As with oral communication, you will tend to be judged less on the content of your message than on its presentation. Are you using a clear, easy-to-read type face and font size, and good quality paper and ink? Use bold characters to give emphasis to key words and phrases rather than underlining, and ensure that there is enough white space around the page.

14. Follow up the reactions

If the communication is an important one, follow it up with a telephone call. Check that the reader really did receive the message you wanted to convey rather than the one the recipient wanted to hear. Ensure that there were no misunderstandings or ambiguities and that the action you needed is under way.

Useful reading

Contemporary business communication, Louis E Boone and David Kurtz, Englewood Cliffs, NJ: Prentice Hall, 1994

Manage the message, Bryan Thresher and Jim Biggin, London: Century Business, 1993

Agreed! How to make your management communication persuasive, Patrick Forsyth, London: Kogan Page, 1993

Putting it across, Angela Haylin, London: Michael Joseph, 1991

Dos and don'ts for effective business writing

Do

- Find, if possible, one or two vivid images or phrases that will convey the key element of your message and make it memorable.
- Establish common ground with your reader and engage their attention and sympathy.
- Be self-critical of your work and be open to other people's comments.

Don't

- Undermine the effectiveness of your communication by spelling or typing mistakes. Always print a page before sending it, and don't rely on the spell checker. Mistakes show up more clearly in black and white than on the screen.
- Suppress arguments that are not wholly supportive or you will alienate readers: confront them and say why you think they are not significant.

Thought starters

- Will a written communication alone be effective in securing what you need to achieve?
- Have you addressed the motivations and concerns of your audience as well as your own?
- Does the communication convey the best possible image of you – and the organisation?

Report Writing

> This checklist is intended both for those new to report writing and for experienced report writers who wish to review their own methods.

MCI Standards

This checklist has relevance for the MCI Management Standards: Key Role D – Manage Information.

Definition

A good report should be readable, interesting and well presented, and it should be no longer than is necessary. It keeps the needs of the readership clearly in mind. As the readers are likely to be busy people who already have a problem reading the material that passes through their hands, a verbose and lengthy document is unlikely to be welcome. A good structure, with clear conclusions and a summary, is vital if an acceptable document is to be produced.

Advantages of good report writing

- Helps you to communicate more effectively.
- Improves your status and your career prospects.
- Contributes to business success by improving communication.
- Creates a good corporate image of the organisation.
- Greatly assists the process of planning and decision making.

Disadvantages of poor report writing

- Time is wasted as readers search for the information they require.
- Readers are frustrated because the information provided is incomplete.
- Misunderstandings result from the lack of clarity in the language used.
- A lack of confidence is felt in both the writer and the message they are trying to put across.
- The report is not read at all.

Action checklist

1. Preparation

Putting pen to paper (or fingers to keyboard) is not the way to start the report writing process. You have to plan what you are going to produce if you want to produce an effective document. In preparing for the actual writing process you should:

- consider the terms of reference or precise purpose. They should define why the report is needed, the type of report it should be, the scope of the subject that is to be covered, and the time scale.
- identify the readership. Is the person who requested the report the primary reader? Who else will see the report? What can the readers be expected to know about the subject? What do they need to know about the subject?
- establish the objectives in your own terms. Present as results to be achieved rather than intentions.

2. Gather and collate the information

With most reports you will not have all the information needed to hand so some form of research or data collection will be required. This may entail identifying and reading other reports, interviewing people, carrying out primary research or drawing together data from a number of different locations. Gathering too much information is not a bad fault; gathering too little definitely is – but bear in mind what you want the information for, otherwise you can bury yourself in a mound of data. Reports are far easier to write when you are able to choose from the information immediately to hand. The important thing is to gain a balanced picture of the subject.

3. Structure your report

Analyse the information to identify that which is most important and that which provides supporting evidence. To achieve this you need to refer back to your terms of reference and your readership. With long documents a detailed outline will be needed. This should link the main subjects with the topics they cover. Consider the order in which you are presenting the information. Restructure them if the order does not seem logical and it fails to portray the message you want.

Plan the layout of your report following the house style of your organisation if applicable. A simple framework for a format can form the basis of most reports. This should include:

- Introduction (to include terms of reference and the methodology)
- Summary
- Main report
- Conclusions

- Recommendations
- Supplementary evidence (including full tables and figures which would obstruct the reading of the main report)

4. Write the report

View your first attempt at putting the report together as a draft. Your plan will provide a broad picture of what you want to achieve. By writing in a single sitting you are far more likely to retain your original concept. Setting yourself a deadline can help to focus the mind.

Make your writing as persuasive as possible by:

- keeping your message simple without oversimplifying
- writing positively, as negative statements are not so easy to understand
- using the active voice, as it is easier to understand than the passive
- including only the information the reader needs to know
- avoiding long and complex sentences, especially those with several subordinate clauses
- using long words only when they are appropriate
- using short words and phrases for conciseness and clarity
- employing technical terms only where they are unavoidable or where you are sure that your audience will understand them. A glossary may be required to assist your readers.

Graphics and visuals are invaluable for expressing complex information. The forms available include tables, line graphs, bar graphs, divided bar graphs, pie charts, pictographs and illustrations; figures are generally to be preferred to tables of data. They should be formatted with care, clearly numbered and titled and introduced within the text. If the graphic is included to help explain a key point it should be placed as close to that point as possible. If it is supplied for documentary support it can be placed at the end of the report. It is often useful to include a simplified or summary figure or table in the main report and to relegate detailed data to an appendix.

5. Review what you have written

You should always allow time to review what you have written, but this should not be done as soon as you have finished writing. Starting the revision a day or two after can be more effective as the ideas are still clear in your mind, but you are fresher to analyse critically what you have written and can view it with more perspective. You will often find simpler and shorter ways of saying what you intend.

Consider whether the report says what you want it to say. Does it fully cover the terms of reference? Analyse the readability of the report, making use of such techniques as Gunning's Fog Index. Check the structure of the report. Check spelling, punctuation and grammatical correctness.

Do your conclusions sufficiently differentiate between those drawn from information presented in the report, your own personal comments and recommendations as to future action based on the report findings?

Ask a colleague to proof-read the report and to consider issues such as ease of understanding and structure.

6. Printing and submission

House style may dictate how your report should be printed and should be followed. For guidance the layout should allow generous margins and make use of a readable typeface. For longer reports starting each section on a new page is advisable.

Aim to submit your report ahead of schedule.

Dos and don'ts for report writing

Do

- Express clearly and concisely what you have to say.
- Provide a summary of the main issues and conclusions.
- Be complete.
- Write with a clear idea of your readership.
- Write with a clear idea of what you are aiming to achieve.

Don't

- Write to impress.
- Include information only because you have found it.

Useful reading

How to write effective reports, 3rd ed, John E Sussams, Aldershot: Gower, 1998
No sweat! The indispensable guide to reports and dissertations, Ray Irving and Cathy Smith, Corby: Institute of Management Foundation, 1998
Persuasive reports and proposals, Andrew Leigh, London: Institute of Personnel and Development, 1997
Successful report writing in a week, Katharine Heritage, London: Hodder & Stoughton, 1997

Thought starters

- When does the report have to be submitted?
- Who is the readership?
- What information do you need?
- Do you understand the brief for the report?
- Should you be following a house style?

Preparing to be Appraised

This checklist describes how the appraisee should prepare for a performance appraisal.

The focus of performance appraisals has shifted in recent years, away from strict evaluation towards improving performance and developing the appraisee by means of an honest and open discussion.

With improvement and development as guiding principles the appraisal process focuses on: results and behaviour not personality; issues and problems not subjective gripes; constructive development to improve performance; and the motivation and growth of the appraisee. It takes place as often as is thought productive, perhaps every three to six months, certainly no less frequently than every twelve.

MCI Standards

This checklist has relevance for the MCI Management Standards: Key Role C – Manage People.

Definition

A performance appraisal is a more complex process than simply a meeting. It usually centres on the key component of a face-to-face discussion wherein one employee's work is discussed, reviewed and appraised by another, using an agreed and understood framework. Usually line managers conduct the appraisal(s) of their staff.

Advantages of performance appraisals

Appraisees should expect to:

- have a clear picture of what is expected of them at the appraisal
- be able to discuss priorities
- gain a platform to remove confusion when overload occurs
- receive feedback on their performance
- be heard and respected
- be offered constructive guidance on attaining agreed goals

- receive help in constructing personal development plans and targets
- accept ownership of their performance.

Requirements for successful appraisal

- Clear understanding of the purpose and the process of the appraisal.
- Clear understanding of the terms of reference of the appraisal – eg if it is linked to pay then what are the evaluation criteria and how are they applied?
- Thorough preparation by the appraisee.
- Resolution to tackle problems honestly.
- Being as relaxed as possible even if past objectives have not been achieved.
- Being purposive, especially in terms of securing agreement to a development proposition.

Action checklist

1. Understand the objectives and terms of reference

If there is an established scheme or programme, then this will provide a framework for action. Make sure you understand that the appraisal scheme is not linked to pay awards – if it isn't. If it is, make sure you understand how the evaluation criteria apply to your work.

2. Agree a date for the appraisal

Much of the hard work of the appraisal should be carried out prior to the meeting itself. While you will require adequate time to prepare information, get your thoughts in order and work out plans for objectives or proposals, don't seek to keep putting it off, as it could assume an overblown importance in your mind.

3. Elicit any specifics

Be clear on any particular objectives that the appraiser wants to cover such as may relate to routine, everyday tasks, or that refer to specific activities, new developments or project work.

4. Prepare for the meeting

Remember that the appraiser – probably your line manager – is (hopefully) unlikely to refer back to specific good or bad episodes or points from the past; they should have been dealt with at the time. The focus is on development, how you may have learned – or not – from the past, and what you are going to do in the future. But you will need to account for things going off course and be able to say how you would do better next time.

5. Account for the past

A starting-point for noting down information is the objectives that were agreed at the last performance appraisal. If there weren't any, it would be useful to clarify this in step 3 above. If there were:

- have you accomplished them within the understood time-frame?
- have you still to accomplish them beyond the time-frame? If so, why?
- have there been problems worthy of mention?
- have there been valuable learning or development points?

6. Ask for feedback

Feedback should be constructive, using events, instances and examples to highlight aspects of learning and development. Asking for feedback can be disconcerting – it can put an unprepared appraiser on the spot, although appraisers should not be unprepared for this. Feedback is invaluable, however, and the key to your appraiser's views on your performance.

7. Don't be reticent about problems

Holding back for fear of offending is as bad as holding forth and casting blame in every quarter but your own. If problems appear ominous and daunting, break them down into approachable discussion points. Try to focus on any difficult issue as a challenge to be resolved, using experience and the appraiser's advice on how to approach the problem in an agreed way.

8. Establish priorities

There will almost certainly have been occasions when you have had to deal with an extremely important (and possibly pressing) task and an urgent staff problem at the same time. The appraisal interview offers an opportunity for discussing such problems and of establishing priorities with your boss. Discussion will not automatically solve them or make them go away, but it can clarify issues and lead to an agreed approach in the future so that you don't, for example, feel pressured into jumping to the loudest shout, but rather tackle what has been agreed as the most important task.

9. Bring departmental relationships into the open

Apart from breakdowns of equipment, systems and people relationships, other departments can cause difficulties. If other departments are a genuine and continuing source of operational or customer difficulty, then raise the question of establishing a service level agreement with them.

10. Propose objectives

Do not go into the appraisal meeting assuming that your boss will have your next year's goals and targets already defined; if you do then s/he probably will. Work out your own proposals, your own tactics and your own targets and remember that you have an advantage that your boss should recognise – you are the one who is doing the job.

11. Agree goals and targets

The setting of goals and targets should not be a one-way process. At worst you can go blindly on 'upping' last year's figures paying no attention to changing resources and changing markets. At best you can discuss a reassessment of factors contributing to change with the appraiser. Do not be afraid to take a completely fresh look: you may need to establish different kinds of goals and targets. There is no point in hitting the bull's eye if the target is the wrong one.

12. Agree further training and development

As well as specific problems and concerns, discuss aspects of continuing development which have not yet been addressed or which form part of a general programme of skills acquisition. Make time to reflect on and plan a flexible development programme from which both your job and you yourself can benefit.

13. Explain personal development requirements

Your boss will help you to identify training needs, some of which may be more obvious than others. Take the opportunity to review your competence and capability, both technically and in terms of general management development.

14. Identify support required

With objectives set and targets agreed, assess whether you need extra support in order to move forward, in terms of training, resources, or even time for further clarification.

15. Agree the evaluation

If the appraisal process has an evaluation element rather than the discussion focus which this checklist has featured, then be clear on what you can contribute to the process and how far the final evaluation is agreed, how far imposed.

16. Do the summing-up

It is good practice for the appraiser to ask the appraisee to summarise the agreed action points and plans from the discussion. While it is important that you 'own' the tasks and activities ahead, it is to your advantage that they are clarified and expressed in a way that you understand. Write up the agreed action points and targets for both you and your boss to sign as a record for the future.

Dos and don'ts for the Appraisee

Do
- Make sure you have enough time to prepare.
- Look upon the appraisal as an opportunity, not a threat.
- Establish some development proposals for discussion.

Don't
- Try to skate around difficult moments.
- Be sold a bum steer without comment if your appraiser goes into monologue-style.
- Spend all your time taking notes – outcomes / action points are important.
- Be over-critical of renegade departments or colleagues.
- Descend to personal levels.

Useful reading

BOOKS
Performance appraisals, Martin Fisher, London: Kogan Page, 1995
Successful appraisals in a week, Di Kamp, London: Hodder & Stoughton, 1998
Appraisal: routes to improved performance, Clive Fletcher, London: Institute of Personnel Management, 1993
Appraising your staff, Philip Moon, London: Kogan Page, 1993

JOURNAL ARTICLES
Being appraised, Trevor Bentley, Training Officer, Vol 31 no 4, May 1995, pp 110–112

Thought starters

- Are you satisfied with your own performance?
- If you have not achieved your set objectives, where does the problem lie?
- When you were last appraised, what went well? What went badly?
- Are you clear on the objectives and the structure of the performance appraisal scheme?
- If you have appraised any of your staff, what have you learned from it?

Handling Conflict Situations

This checklist examines the approach to personal conflict and is designed to help line managers handle conflict when it arises.

Conflict can arise from a host of roots and causes but principally it will occur from differences between people, over ideas and through various situations. 'Ideas conflict' can be both desirable and creative when handled constructively; 'situations' can cause frustration and resentment if not dealt with; 'personal conflicts' can be damaging and destructive unless managed with thought and care. Ultimately conflict can cost a great deal of time and money. Most organisations and individuals recognise the need to solve personal conflicts before they become destructive.

MCI Standards

This checklist has relevance for the MCI Management Standards: Key Role C – Manage People.

Definition

Personal conflict occurs when two or more parties have opposing attitudes or approaches to a particular situation, issue or person. Obvious sources of conflict range from a difference of opinion, problematic working conditions or unrealistic work expectations through discriminatory behaviour (such as racism or sexism), to poor communication or non-compliance with organisational norms or values.

There are situations where an ethical or practical issue emerges that you know should be confronted. Here, conflict can be positive – you may even have to create it temporarily. For example, a member of staff turns up late every day and the manager fails to confront the individual. This avoidance, may in future lead to a development of conflict through frustration and resentment in the other team members.

Conflict can occur between a member of staff and the manager, between two or more members of a team, or between departments, sections or managers.

Whether you are involved directly affects whether you negotiate with someone else, apply grievance or disciplinary measures or mediate between other parties.

Conflict can be covert and take the form of resentment from a team member passed over for promotion or irritation caused by an individual's personal habits. Such conflict is much harder to detect and easier to ignore. Whichever type it is, all conflict still needs to be managed before it becomes a destructive force.

Advantages

The advantages of managing conflict situations are:

- better motivated staff; staff energies are directed to work rather than emotions
- an organisation or staff that presents a positive image to the outside world
- improved team work
- better personal development of individuals.

Disadvantages

The disadvantages of avoiding or failing to manage a conflict situation may include:

- it will fester and may spread to others
- staff energies become dissipated
- misdirected energies contribute to falling productivity
- inaction may be the easy option in the short term, but the problem ultimately will be harder to solve.

Action checklist

1. Recognise conflict

To handle conflict you have to spot it. Remember it can be overt – from an obvious or identifiable cause, clearly visible and defined, or covert – from a less obvious cause, hidden and with a potentially unrelated root source (eg a member of staff could apparently be in conflict with colleagues, when the real root cause is their perception that a supervisor's treatment of them is discriminatory).

2. Monitor the climate

Monitoring the climate at work gives you an early warning system, which makes it far easier to deal with conflict swiftly and efficiently before it gets out of hand. This does not mean constantly being on your guard; it simply means being prepared and keeping your eyes open. If you see a likely conflict situation, don't turn a blind eye. Early action saves time and stress later.

3. Research the situation

Take time to find out the real cause of the conflict, who is involved, what the key issue is, and what its actual and potential effects are. Empathise – see the situation from other people's point of view rather than come to snap judgements.

4. Plan the approach

Don't take sides. Instead, encourage the parties concerned to examine the interests behind their position and try to create a climate of exchange so that the parties may deal with each other more constructively next time. Work out a strategy based on what this investigation has shown. Managers should decide upon the result they want to achieve, bearing in mind that, as different evidence emerges, this outcome may not always be possible.

5. Handle the issue

Stay in control of the situation. Handling conflict is a difficult process which can create extreme emotions. Use the following techniques.

- Stay calm – take time to respond, don't give a knee-jerk reaction. If necessary take a rain check until everyone involved is calm enough to discuss the issues rationally and constructively.

- Listen to the points of view of all involved and take time to understand all the issues involved in the conflict. It is important to remember that people will be more open and honest if they feel they have a receptive and interested audience. Think about your body language and spoken language.

- Avoid **fight** or **flight**. The instinctive human reaction to conflict is either to run away, or face it and fight. Neither of these approaches is constructive.

  Flight avoids solving the conflict and leads to loss of respect.

  Fighting back or being aggressive to one or both parties when you are not personally involved causes greater long term conflict and intimidates staff.

- Stay assertive – this means avoiding being either passive or aggressive; neither is assertive, and each is a short term approach unlikely to solve the conflict.

Passive behaviour = apologising, withdrawn body language, always accepting the other person's point of view whether it is right or not.

Aggressive behaviour = being authoritarian, rarely listening to reasoned argument.

An assertive approach is generally the best way to handle conflict and it means:

- acknowledging the views and rights of all parties
- encouraging the parties to find the causes of the conflict – and solutions
- trying to ensure that opinions and thoughts are expressed honestly and openly
- suggesting a constructive way forward.

6. Let everyone have their say

If you have managed to get the parties around a table for discussion in a climate where exchange is possible then a compromise solution may now be feasible. Remember that your desired solution must hit a wide range of targets. It must:

- help to build good working relationships
- be legitimate, non-discriminatory and compatible with organisational practice
- recognise all parties' alternatives
- help to improve communication
- help to generate a lasting commitment to the solution.

7. Find the way forward

The most important aspect of handling a conflict situation is to find an acceptable way forward. Examine the options and decide what to do next. Can you reach a compromise acceptable to both, or all, sides? If not, what action needs to be taken to prevent the conflict from continuing? Make sure everyone knows what the conclusion is and what they are expected to do.

The next steps need to be agreed and spelled out – it could be an individual's need for counselling, the likelihood of disciplinary proceedings or an agreement to be followed (even moving a member of staff to another department if there is a deep-rooted personal antagonism). Sometimes there may be problems relating to health or psychology – you have to judge where your limits lie in resolving apparently intractable personal antagonisms.

8. Appraise – don't dwell

It is important to learn from conflict situations and move forward. Don't dwell on the past and re-open old wounds.

Appraise the conflict and the way it was handled. Decide what can be learned from this. How can similar conflicts be avoided in the future? How could it be handled better next time? Learn from the experience – and keep your eye on what has been resolved, to stop it flaring up again.

Dos and don'ts for handling a conflict situation

Do
- Tackle conflict early, to avoid it escalating.
- Think it through and plan how to deal with the conflict.
- Refrain from offering your own opinion before understanding the full picture.
- Try to avoid instinctive reactions.
- Stay assertive.

Don't
- Take it personally (unless it is personal), it is a fact of life.
- Avoid the issue and ignore the conflict.
- Fight anger with anger.
- Jump in without assessing and understanding the problem.
- Run away.
- Handle conflict in public.

Useful reading

BOOKS

Curing conflict, Leslie P Lewis and Institute of Management, London: Pitman, 1994

Constructive conflict management: managing to make a difference, John Crawley, London: Nicholas Brealey, 1992

A sudden outbreak of common sense: managing conflict through mediation, Andrew Floyer Acland, London: Hutchinson Business Press, 1990

Managing disagreement constructively, Herbert S Kindler, London: Kogan Page, 1988

JOURNAL ARTICLES

Conflicts of interest, Lynne Irvine, British Journal of Administrative Management, March / April 1998, pp8–10

How to turn conflict to your advantage, Roy Holder, Works Management, March 1997, pp28–30

Thought starters

To resolve conflict, do you:

- encourage all parties to explore factors common to their respective positions?
- try to enable the parties to deal effectively with their differences?
- try to make it easier for the parties to deal with each other next time?
- encourage the parties to come up with ways of generating mutual gain?
- encourage parties to work out realistic appraisals of their point of view?
- facilitate questioning of inflexible attitudes?
- know which skills you need to work on?

Managing (your Relationship with) your Boss

This checklist is for those who wish, or need, to manage the relationship with their boss more effectively.

The relationship a manager has with his/her boss is of fundamental importance to their ability to perform and develop well within their role. This relationship needs to be planned and developed. It is not simply a case of being pleasant or getting along well together – it has to be a conscious act. Essentially then, what you are managing is the relationship – not the individual.

MCI Standards

This checklist has relevance for the MCI Management Standards: Key Role C – Manage People.

Definition

A good working relationship between you and your boss should enable you to develop your skills, knowledge and career and combine:

- fairness
- mutual respect
- trust and rapport
- openness and honesty in communication.

Managing your boss is about constructing a relationship of mutual trust, respect and support. It means acknowledging who is boss but maintaining the freedom within this relationship to do the best for the organisation, the team and yourself.

The key word here is 'manage'; it implies an active on-going process and not a one-off activity.

Advantages

There are great advantages to managing your relationship with your boss:

- it's the most important working relationship you have – make the most of it
- it creates a productive and communicative working relationship
- it ensures each of you knows what is possible and feasible, en route to achieving the results that matter to you both
- a good working relationship improves your self-esteem
- it aids your personal development
- it helps you overcome problems or conflict when they arise.

Disadvantages

There are no real disadvantages to managing the relationship, but there are disadvantages to not doing so. Fail to manage the relationship with your boss and it:

- can create a manipulative relationship where office politics or personal style dominates the way you and your boss work together
- can hinder open communication
- can make you lose self-esteem
- can make problems or conflict harder to solve
- can lead to feelings that you are on opposing sides – or at least not on exactly the same team.

Action checklist

1. Communicate properly ...

... on time, in adequate detail and regularly; make sure formal communication works, but also ensure you simply talk and compare notes from time to time. Prevention is better than cure, and effective communication prevents a lot of misunderstandings and breakdowns in relationships.

2. Identify any blockages

Examine your current relationship with your boss. Identify where the blockages to a good working relationship lie – perhaps you have trouble communicating, or find it hard to express your own opinions or have discussions about workload. Identify what triggers these problems. Also think about parts of the relationship that work well. Build upon these and work on cutting problems in other areas.

3. Identify your boss's key objectives and values

Think about what is important to your boss and work hard on these areas. The two main areas to pay attention to are:

- his/her objectives – what, in the eyes of your manager, are the key objectives and what support can you give towards achieving them?
- what personal values your boss holds dear – for instance customer care. Work on supporting these values and don't do things that are contrary to them. Be wary, however, of evidently self-interested values, such as personal status.

4. Clarify boundaries of responsibility

Sort out with your boss exactly what decisions you can make

- after discussion with your boss
- on your own but reporting to your boss afterwards
- on your own with no need to report.

Lack of clarity can be a major source of conflict and friction.

5. Tackle the simple issues

Look through the problems you have identified and decide which are the simple issues to solve. Can small administrative problems be solved by introducing a simple new system? Discuss minor sensitivities (eg opening the office window, working in silence or with background noise) with your boss and try to reach a compromise. But don't relay your mastery of trivia when your boss would expect you to deal with them as routine – don't waste time reporting unimportant successes.

Work overload is often a common cause of conflict. Don't take on work you can't manage – be honest but remember your manager's objectives and always suggest an alternative solution.

6. Tackle longer term issues with assertiveness

Some blockages can't be removed overnight. Concentrate on building up a stronger relationship with your boss. This means being assertive but not aggressive. Express your point of view, respect your boss's opinions and work to find mutually acceptable solutions to existing problems. This will improve the value of your relationship and help you to handle difficult situations more effectively in the future. Don't loop the system by going over your boss's head – however attractive this may seem. If you feel blocked, tackle the issues directly to avoid creating other problems later.

7. Value yourself

Don't underestimate yourself or your point of view. If you don't have faith in your ability to do a good job and develop in your role, your boss certainly won't.

8. Focus on loyalty and support

Concentrate on supporting the weak spots in your boss's make up without making it too obvious you are doing so. Find out what parts of the business they enjoy and are good at, and those s/he doesn't like doing or perhaps doesn't have the skills to deal with. Make yourself indispensable. Show you are keen to learn skills which complement your boss's skills. Win their trust by achieving things they value. Together you can become a winning team.

9. Think about how other people see you

People can assume a lot about your abilities from the way you look or the way you present yourself. They may think a scruffy, sullen looking person is disorganised, bad at their job and generally unreliable. Look smart. Smile and act positive.

10. Celebrate success

Celebrate your successes. Make sure your manager knows when you have done well and that your success is theirs too.

11. Seize on opportunities

Keep your eye on the big picture and not just the task in hand. Don't use an overload of work as an excuse to avoid activities such as attending conferences or meeting senior directors. Weigh up the short-term disbenefits against the potential longer-term value for the organisation. Think about what these opportunities do for your development and what you could learn.

12. Communicate your agenda

There's no need to be abrasive, but a modicum of repetition may be useful in making sure that your agenda gets heard. This may relate to specific projects or on-going work but think about the bigger picture too. What do you want to learn? Where do you want your career to go? Instead of always playing your boss's tune, develop joint objectives.

13. Review issues and actions, and plan future development

Appraise issues which are important to you and discuss them with your manager. They are actually important to them too, because if you fail, your boss fails. Discuss problems before they get out of hand and have some ideas for solutions ready to talk through.

14. Nip conflict in the bud

If conflict breaks out between you and your boss – handle it. Don't run away from it or tackle anger with anger.

15. Review the relationship

Sit down from time to time and ask 'How are we doing?'. Focus on the relationship so that you both know where things stand, and can work to improve and maintain the underlying relationship between you. If a conflict – or a particularly successful joint approach – has occurred, use it as a vehicle for reviewing the relationship and work out what to do again in future and what to do differently next time.

Dos and don'ts for managing your boss

Do

- Make the time and take the trouble to talk to each other.
- Form an alliance – understand your manager's objectives and values.
- Remind your boss (and yourself) that you are on the same side.
- Learn to support the weaker areas of your manager's style.
- Be wary of gimmicks like encouraging your boss to think your idea was his/hers.
- Appraise and review your current work, future goals and the relationship.

Don't

- Be passive – always doing what your manager wants and not putting forward your own viewpoint.
- Be aggressive – fighting fire with fire rarely works.
- Go over your boss's head if you can avoid it.
- Ignore problems and avoid discussing them.

Useful reading

BOOKS

Militant managers: how to spot, how to work with, how to manage your highly aggressive boss, Carol Elbing and Alvar Elbing, Burr Ridge: Irwin, 1994
Coping with difficult bosses, Robert Bramson, London: Nicholas Brealey, 1993
How to deal with difficult people, Ursula Markham, London: Thorsons, 1993
How to manage your boss and survive the system, Derek Rowntree, London: Sphere, 1989

JOURNAL ARTICLE

Managing your boss, John J Gabarro and John P Kotter, Harvard Business Review, vol 71 no 3, May/June 1993, pp150–157

Thought starters

- Are you clear about your manager's objectives and values?
- Are you clear where your relationship is already good and bad?
- Are you assertive with your manager?
- Successful relationships are based on communication – how good are your communications with your manager, in terms of timeliness, frequency, quality and coverage?
- Have you 'classified' your boss into a 'category'?

Counselling your
Colleagues

This checklist is designed for managers who, in the context of their roles, may be required to help their colleagues through the use of counselling skills.

To become a professional counsellor can take several years' training and supervised practical experience. Few managers have this level of qualification, but many of the skills employed by counsellors can be put to use in a work situation.

MCI Standards

This checklist has relevance for the MCI Management Standards: Key Role C – Manage People.

Definition

Handled successfully, counselling is a process which helps an individual clarify their motivations, worries and hopes; helps them to come to terms with their feelings, and enables them to take responsibility for, and begin to resolve, their difficulties.

Counselling is not a process of advice-giving, nor does it involve the counsellor providing or managing solutions to the problems experienced by the 'client'.

Action checklist

1. Check your organisation's personnel policies to ensure that by offering counselling you conform to these

Some organisations have formal arrangements for counselling and it is important not to disregard these.

2. Ensure that you have a suitable room in which counselling can take place

It is essential to choose somewhere which is quiet, free from interruption and appropriate to the nature of the problem. Ensure you will not be disturbed by using an 'Engaged' sign on the door, and divert your telephone to avoid interruptions.

- Try to avoid a formal office setting with a desk between you and your colleague.
- If you need to keep an unobtrusive eye on the time, position a clock somewhere appropriate (ie not behind your seat).

3. Ensure there is sufficient time for the meeting

If you know you must end your meeting at a particular time, inform your colleague of this at the outset. To avoid too little time being available for the session it is often more sensible to book a meeting (perhaps only a day in advance). Even if there is no need for a time limit, it is often useful to set one of about an hour to prevent the discussion merely going over the same ground again and again.

4. Address your feelings towards your colleague

Before the meeting, it is essential to confront your personal feelings towards your colleague and put them to one side. Whether or not you like your colleague is irrelevant.

5. Open the meeting by explaining the framework

At the beginning of the counselling session it is essential to lay down some ground-rules. These may include:

- **what the expectations of the discussion should be** – ie you will not be able to provide advice or guidance or solve any problems for your colleague
- **time limitations** – state again what these are, and whether you will offer a follow-up session if needed
- **note taking** – stress any notes taken are for your own use and will not be revealed to a third party

- **confidentiality** – assure your colleague that matters of confidentiality will be treated as such, as they may be reticent through fear of being regarded as something of a risk in the future. Explain the only exception to this will be if you both agree that something needs to be discussed with another party.

6. Begin to explore the issues with your colleague

There can be no set-in-stone format for counselling as each session is dependent on the needs of the individual. However, the following skills are all essential to enable the issues to be explored.

- **Actively listen** – What does your colleague feel? What is their point of view? What do they view as happening to them? What do they do (or not do)? It is essential to understand that the view of the facts or situation that your colleague has will be more important to them than the facts themselves – and that their behaviour may not reflect their true feelings. By rephrasing the concerns expressed by your colleague you demonstrate that you have listened to what is being said and at the same time can seek clarification of the issues involved. Summarising what has been said occasionally throughout the conversation helps both parties remain focused.

- **Empathise** – Empathy is not the same as sympathy. Empathy means you recognise and understand the issues by which your colleague feels confronted without having to take their side or agree totally with what they are saying. Empathy can help to encourage your colleague to be more honest and exact when describing the issues.

- **Question** – There are many reasons for questions, and many types of questions. In a counselling situation questions may enable you to clarify your understanding of the issues, will help to focus on areas you think may be important and can demonstrate your interest in the other person.

  Open, closed and delving types of questions are all of value in a counselling situation. Open questions can help your colleague begin to talk about an issue, and can provide you with information on how they feel. Closed questions help you to establish precise facts but tend to lead to very short answers. Delving questions enable you to probe an issue more fully and can help to draw out the whole picture.

- **Challenge** – By challenging statements made, your colleague is forced to consider their situation more closely. It is useful to challenge if it appears that they are dragging the discussion round in circles, if they have an unrealistic self-image (either too positive or more usually too negative) or if they appear to contradict themselves.

  Challenging statements may be based on phrases such as:

'You say that you are struggling with your current project, yet I see you as meeting all its objectives and time-scales. Why do you think there is a difference in our views?'

7. Recognise situations which are beyond your help

In certain circumstances it may be necessary to refer your colleague on to other organisations or counsellors who may be better equipped to help. Be aware of sources of information which may provide contact details (local telephone book or local reference library). The personnel department may have some details, but be sure not to break a confidence if you speak to them.

8. Help your colleague in the area of problem-solving

Counselling does not mean that the counsellor provides solutions to the issues raised by the colleague. It does, however, involve the counsellor in the process of problem-solving. From the discussion, the problem area will have been identified, as will possible causes. It is now necessary for the individual to set specific objectives to enable them to tackle the problem and assign timescales and means of monitoring their progress.

9. Close the session in an appropriate manner

Summarise what has been discussed and what actions have been agreed upon, and where appropriate arrange a follow up session.

Dos and don'ts for counselling

Do
- Clarify what the realistic expectations of a counselling session should be.
- Assure your colleague of confidentiality.
- Encourage your colleague to:
  – explore their concern or problem
  – clarify the issue
  – set objectives for action.

Don't
- Let personal feelings intrude on the discussion.
- Take on the responsibility for solving problems.
- Be directive in what you say.

Useful reading
Handbook of counselling in organizations, Michael Carroll and Michael Walton, London: Sage, 1997
The IPD guide on counselling at work, London: Institute of Personnel and Development, 1997

Counselling for managers, Nigel MacLennan, Aldershot: Gower, 1996
Counselling in the workplace, Jenny Summerfield and Lyn Van Oudtshoorn, London:
Institute of Personnel and Development, 1995
Counselling techniques for managers, Hilary Walmsley, London: Kogan Page, 1994

Useful addresses
British Association of Counselling, 1 Regent Place, Rugby, Warwickshire, CV21 2PJ, Tel:
01788 550899
Employee Assistance Professionals Association, c/o Richard Hopkins, President, APE
Britannic Chapter, Pinnacle Counselling Ltd, 2 Dovedale Studios, 465 Battersea Park
Road, London, SW11 4LN
Relate National Marriage Guidance, Herbert Grey College, Little Church Street, Rugby,
Warwickshire, CV21 3AP, Tel: 01788 573241

Thought starters

- The greater the perceived level of listening, the more likely the individual
  will be to accept comments and contributions from you.
- Repeating problems do not solve themselves.

Networking

This checklist is designed to help you to develop your business networking skills, in order to retain and gain customers and suppliers, and to expand your range of beneficial contacts.

MCI Standards

This checklist has relevance for the MCI Management Standards: Key Roles A and B – Manage Activities and Manage Resources.

Definition

The term 'networking' produces different responses from different people. As an activity, networking is not new. It is a well-established activity which has attracted a new label.

Our networks embrace the range of informal and formal relationships in which we are involved; networking implies an awareness of our networks and of their potential value both to ourselves and to other members.

Networks overlap; A and B may be in the same network but each will have contacts in other networks. Our networks are not static – if we use them, they constantly expand, but if we neglect them, they shrink.

Networks are generally of four kinds – personal, organisational, professional and strategic. All provide access to information, development opportunities, support and influence.

Benefits of networking

Networking enables you to:

- improve and extend the quality of your relationships
- create opportunities to meet more potential customers
- be better informed and share information with fellow network members
- share in your customers' social interests, thus enhancing your business relationships
- meet your peers in other organisations.

Disadvantages of networking

Networks don't just happen: they require the investment of those rare commodities, time and energy. They also require a disposition to give as well as take. Most of us are happy to do this; for the minority who are not, networking may be an embarrassment.

Action checklist

1. Prepare for your networking

Networking is an activity and a skill which requires planning if it is to succeed. Remember the aim of networking (in the present context) is to improve your business potential. Spend some time identifying networks of which you would like to be a member. Are you interested in 'talking shops' which may be sources of new contacts, or in situations which may provide opportunities for self-development, or as a step on the road to the development of your business?

2. Identify formal networks and develop relationships with them

Professional Institutes and Associations run local activities and help you to keep up-to-date with technical developments. They inform you about successes and 'best practice' in your line of business and provide support for your continuing professional development.

Trade Associations help you to keep up-to-date with new products and industry trends, and can help to identify opportunities for the future.

Training and Enterprise Councils (TECs)/Local Enterprise Companies (LECs) are bodies with remits to develop training and expertise in their local areas. The objectives of TECs usually include securing the commitment of employers to improve the education and training of their employees and to foster enterprise in the local community. Management Development meetings organised by TECs are usually free of charge, and business expansion advice is also readily available.

Business Links aim to improve the competitiveness of local firms by bringing together local support organisations, such as TECs and Chambers of Commerce, to develop the full range of services focused on customer needs and delivered from a single point of access. Personal Business Advisers will visit you and help you to plan the development and running of your business. Some services are free of charge. Open meetings encourage business people to get together.

Business Clubs are often focused on small businesses, where members have similar ideas and problems. Meetings are usually informal and activities promote contact between members to generate business between them.

Chambers of Industry and Commerce provide information on a wide range of business activities in your area. Chambers have links with Training and Enterprise Councils/Local Enterprise Companies, Business Links and the Department of Trade and Industry. They hold social events to help you establish and build on personal relationships with customers and suppliers. Many local Chambers offer continuous programmes of training courses and seminars.

3. Identify informal networks

These include:

- sports and social clubs
- neighbourhood organisations and community groups
- voluntary organisations.

The range of such organisations varies from town to town and from area to area.

4. Take steps to foster your networks

Consider what networks you belong to and the range of your contacts in each. Who could help you? Whom could you help? Build up a record to which you can refer. Consider how you propose to develop your networks.

Take stock. What do you want from your network? Are you looking for a regular flow of information, opportunities to develop yourself and your business, support, access to influence, or opportunities to become influential? What, in turn, can you contribute? What are you prepared to contribute?

Learn how to behave in ways that are consistent with networking ethics. Be open-minded; keep your promises; treat others in the way in which you would like to be treated; and ask for and give help without embarrassment. Most of all, don't forget to acknowledge help. A smile and a thankyou are beyond price.

How will you go about networking? What style of approach suits you best? Michelli and Straw suggest that there are three styles:

Conscious networkers have clear-cut goals. They recognise what is missing in their networks and set out to identify those who will meet their needs and to meet and develop relationships with them. The approach of conscious networkers is systematic and calculating.

Open networkers are again calculating but tend to take a longer-term view, building networks with the future in mind. Their objectives may be less clear-cut than those of intuitive networkers but they recognise those who may be useful in the future and cultivate relationships with them.

Intuitive networkers are neither systematic nor calculating. They enjoy mixing with people and do so as a matter of course. They are 'good with people' and may even be unaware of the extent of their range of contacts or of their potential value in a business context.

5. Get down to practicalities

● **Design your business card to project you and your business**
Think of all the factors – colour, logo, taste, positive messages – that will help to make people remember your business. There are two sides to your business card, so consider listing some of your services on the reverse side. If you export/import, carry bilingual cards – it will make it easier for your foreign customer/supplier to network with you.

● **Describe your business in a nutshell**
Prepare a clean, short, introductory statement which describes you and your business. If it's more than two sentences long you will lose the listener's attention. Adapt the statement to the person you are talking to – this will prevent it sounding too rehearsed. Use humour if you feel people will be comfortable. It can relax the atmosphere and encourage other people to join in the conversation. But do keep what you have to say brief – no one wants to listen to a long, tedious diatribe about how wonderful your business is. Be brief and let the facts speak for themselves.

● **Prepare a brochure**
If you prepare a brochure describing your products/services, make sure it is in plain English, free from jargon. Clear statements, with plenty of white space, are more effective than a cluttered brochure with lots of colour in it. Remember to convey the message – simply and straightforwardly – that you care about your customers and wish to meet their needs, not just to sell them what you have to offer.

● **Get to meetings/events in good time**
The sooner you get there, the more chance you have to arrange things to your advantage. If there is an opportunity to display your brochures, set out a few for people to pick up. If name badges are available, wear one. Having your own is useful, as event badges often use small print. When you are introduced to new people, let them do the talking to begin with. You will learn about them, what interests them, what is concerning them. Encourage them to talk about their business and their future plans. This information will help you to decide how to develop the new relationship. Don't stay too long with each person. Offer your business card, and suggest you might talk again later. Keep the other person's card in a separate pocket to the one in which you have yours, or you may find yourself handing out someone else's card.

● **Offer help**

Offer to help if you wish to meet someone again to discuss business. It signals a clear message of service, rather than of blatantly wanting a person's custom.

● **Listen to people's contributions**

Business presentations at meetings can be ideal for picking up a possible lead – people often express their problems to a group, rather than confide only in their business partners. You may also identify competitors who could benefit from a partnership arrangement.

● **Generate a record for each contact**

Set some time aside each week to chase up contacts – regular contact with people will encourage them to think about you and possibly steer business in your direction.

● **Make notes after informal meetings**

You can't easily make notes while talking to people, but you can often jot down a key word which you can expand on afterwards – immediately afterwards, while your memory is still fresh.

Useful reading

Networking (Management Directions), Dena Michelli and Fiona McWilliams, Corby: The Institute of Management Foundation, 1996

Successful networking in a week, Dena Michelli and Alison Straw, London: Hodder & Stoughton, 1995

Working for yourself: the Daily Telegraph guide to self-employment, 15th ed, Godfrey Golzen, London: Kogan Page, 1994

Thought starters

● People buy from people, so your customers are part of your network.
● Talk about their problems and how you can help; they don't want to know about yours.
● Recall some point from the last conversation you had with X. It may help X to remember you.

Working out your Redundancy Package

> **This checklist is designed as a guide for those working out their redundancy package.**

MCI Standards

This checklist has relevance for the MCI Management Standards: Key Role C – Manage People.

Definition

In broad terms, a job is redundant if:

- your employers are ceasing to carry on the business which employs you
- your employers are closing down the business at the site where you work, eg if a company with four distribution centres decides to close one down
- your employers are transferring the business from the site where you work to another location, eg a company with two offices decides to rationalise on to one site
- your employers need fewer employees to do your particular kind of work, eg they decide to have one manager responsible for sales instead of two
- your employers need fewer employees to do your particular kind of work at the place where you work, eg the divisional personnel function is closed but the head office personnel function remains and a personnel manager is appointed for each site.

The basic test of redundancy is whether your employer now needs fewer employees, either across the company or at a particular location. In theory the amount of work need not have changed but it must be capable of being done by fewer people.

Action checklist

1. Check eligibility

To be eligible for the statutory minimum redundancy payment you must meet all the following criteria:

- be employed under a contract of service (ie not self employed)
- be under the normal retirement age in the company for the kind of role, or if there is no normal retirement age, be under 65
- have at least two years' service with the current employers, including any employment with associated employers. (Years before age 18 do not count).

Certain groups of employees are excluded from statutory redundancy pay, for example those who normally work overseas (even if their employers are based in the United Kingdom). Also, case law has established that employees who volunteer for early retirement in a redundancy situation may be ineligible for redundancy pay.

2. Calculate your payment

The amount of the payment is calculated in relation to age, length of service and 'a week's pay'.

Completed years of service	Amount of payment
Numbers of years service between age 18–21	0.5 week's pay per year
Numbers of years service between age 22–40	1 week's pay per year
Numbers of years service over 41, up to age 64	1.5 weeks' pay per year

If you are paid an annual salary a week's pay will be 1/52nd of your current annual salary. There is an upper limit on 'a week's pay' which is revised each year. The current (April 1998) figure is £220, making the maximum statutory payment £6600. The formula for arriving at this is 20 (years) × 1.5 (weeks) × £220. The maximum length of service which can be taken into account in a redundancy pay claim is 20 years. This means that if you earn more than £220, then your redundancy pay will be calculated as if you earned £220 per week. Benefits such as company cars do not count.

Employers must give a statement setting out how redundancy payment has been calculated. A ready reckoner which will help you to calculate the number of weeks' pay due is contained within the DTI publication – Redundancy Payments PL808.

Of course, many redundancy payments are substantially in excess of the statutory minimum. However, payments often preserve the age/service bias of the statutory payment in some form.

3. Negotiating your package

Explore the possibility of negotiating. Many packages may be increased because of individuals negotiating for additional benefits such as:

- car
- outplacement support
- career counselling
- access to secretarial facilities
- health insurance.

It may also be possible to negotiate an additional lump sum payment if the circumstances of the termination of your employment indicate the possibility of a claim for compensation for unfair dismissal (see 6 below).

4. Tax position

Traditionally the first £30,000 of all payments received was tax free. However, the Inland Revenue is now much harsher on which payments actually qualify for this exemption and professional advice should be sought. Statutory redundancy payments are tax free, but may have to be included within the £30,000 exemption limit.

Any payments over £30,000 will be taxable in full. The most substantial payment people normally receive is salary in lieu of notice and this is taxable.

Those who feel they have been taxed unfairly can challenge the decision with their employers or the Tax Office.

5. Employers' responsibilities

If you are made redundant, there is no need for you to put in a claim for redundancy pay as it is your employer's responsibility to calculate it and make payment. If, however, you do not receive the redundancy pay to which you think you are entitled, you should make a written request to your employer, or alternatively you may make a claim to an Industrial Tribunal. You must make any such claims within 6 months of the date of the termination of your employment.

6. Unfair dismissal

True redundancy is a fair reason for dismissal but there are a number of circumstances in which an employee who is made redundant can sue for unfair dismissal eg where someone other than you should have been selected for redundancy. If you feel that you have a case seek legal advice.

Dos and don'ts for working out your redundancy package

Do

- Seek professional advice.
- Negotiate for additional benefits.
- Understand the tax implications of your package.

Don't

- Automatically accept the first offer.

Useful reading

BOOKS AND LEAFLETS

Redundancy payments, Department for Trade and Industry, Leaflet PL808

Guidance through redundancy, Institute of Management, Corby

Compensation and remedies, London: Incomes Data Services, 1997 (States law as at 30 November 1997)

Redundancy employment law handbook, London: Incomes Data Services, 1996, (States law as at 30 July 1996)

JOURNAL ARTICLE

1998 IRS redundandy survey part two, IRS Employment Review, No 659, July 1998, pp9–16 (purple)

Useful addresses

Career Advisory Service, Institute of Management, Cottingham Road, Corby, Northants, NN17 1TT, Tel: 01536 204222, (Members are entitled to one free telephone consultation with the Institute's solicitors – Royds Treadwell. Telephone for details.)

DTI Redundancy Payments Service. Floor 7–9, Hagley House, 83–85 Hagley Road, Birmingham, B16 8QG, Tel: 0121 456 4411

P.O. Box 15, Exchange House, 60 Exchange Road, Watford, Herts, WD1 7SP, Tel: 01923 210700

Advisory Conciliation and Arbitration Service (ACAS), Brandon House, 180 Borough High Street, London, SE1 1LW, Tel: 0171 210 3000

Thought starters

- Be prepared to bargain – employers are sometimes far more generous than you would expect.
- Some settlements may not be as attractive as they seem – seek advice.

Redundancy: The Next Day

This checklist aims to help anticipate the trauma of redundancy and to face its psychological and practical problems in a positive way. It is intended for the potentially redundant employee, not the employer. There was a time when redundancy was something which happened to other people. Many of us – perhaps the majority – expected to remain with the same employer throughout our careers. In today's fast-changing world, life-long employment with the same organisation seems less and less likely. Redundancy can happen to anyone and by acknowledging the possibility now, should the worst happen, we will be better able to cope with it.

MCI Standards

This checklist has relevance for the MCI Management Standards: Key Role C – Manage People.

Definition

A job is considered to be redundant if the employer:

- is ceasing to carry on the business the employment is in
- is closing down the business at the site at which the job is based
- is transferring the business from the site where the employment is based to another location
- requires fewer employees to do the type of work
- needs fewer employees to carry out the work at the place where it is carried out (eg the divisional personnel function is closed but head office personnel remains and a personnel manager is appointed for each site).

Advantages of anticipating redundancy

- You have a plan of campaign which can be put into effect without delay.
- The shock of redundancy may be reduced, thus enabling you to react positively more quickly.

- You can see redundancy, if it occurs, as a challenge to be met head-on rather than as a blow to your self-esteem.

Action checklist

1. Recognise that you are in a state of shock

However much you may have expected it, the final news that you have been made redundant has almost certainly left you in a state of shock. A series of psychological transitional stages have to be gone through before the new situation becomes accepted.

Expect to feel a sense of loss of familiar places, people, habits and routines and a loss of the sense of competence which you have been used to enjoying and, perhaps, of influence, power and authority. Expect to experience a wide range of emotions, all of which are manifestations of difficulty in accepting the shock of change, and to want to act as if it is 'business as usual' and as if nothing has changed. You are the same person that you were a week ago, feeling a normal range of emotions in the circumstances. Up until now, 'redundancy could happen to anyone': now it has happened to you.

2. Take action but don't make decisions

You are probably in a highly emotional state so the 'day after' should be a day for action – and don't forget exercise and fresh air. Don't pretend that you are thinking when, in fact, you are doing no more than feeling sorry for yourself. Avoid making decisions. You are in no condition to do so and the danger is that if you allow yourself to make decisions they will be dramatic and irrational and not based on good judgement.

3. Forget 'Why me?'

This is the first reaction of many who have suffered the pain of redundancy. They cannot understand why they were the one chosen to be made redundant, rather than someone else. Recognise that such speculation changes nothing and only deters you from taking the action needed to counter your new situation. 'Why me?' only makes sense if you avoid comparisons with others; if you sit down with someone with whom you can speak frankly; and if you consider, as objectively as possible, how and in what circumstances you might have presented yourself to better advantage. The only point in such analysis is to help you to resolve to change in the future and not to confine yourself to regret, and, as with decision making, it should not take place in the immediate aftermath of redundancy. It often helps to pretend you are giving advice to someone else in the same position – this 'objectifies' the situation (we are all good at advising others).

4. Don't pretend

Make no pretences to anyone. Like many before you, and many now, you are redundant and looking for a new job. Be dignified but don't try to pretend to the world that nothing has changed. There is no shame in redundancy. It has happened to thousands of others.

5. Find another job (a job in itself)

Treat your search as a job itself. Subject yourself to regular hours. Take only a reasonable period for lunch. Be professional about it. Keep a daily record of what you have done; keep a diary which will tell you what leads you must follow up and when. You may no longer be selling your former employer's products or services but you are selling something far more valuable – yourself.

6. Identify sources of help

List all the people who may be able to help you with their names, titles, addresses and telephone numbers. Include any outplacement services provided by your former employer. Don't start calling contacts immediately, and when you do call avoid giving them a 'hard luck story'. They may be bored or embarrassed and the word may spread. Wait until you are composed and can be professional and dignified – but don't forget to display becoming humility. You need their help so don't resort to arrogance as a cover for your inner feelings. Have specific objectives in mind rather than asking for 'any help at all'.

7. Locate sources of job advertisements

Go to the library (where most of the quality press is available for free reference) and find out which newspapers and periodicals contain advertisements for the type of job in which you may be interested. Note the day on which each is published and record it in your diary. Don't forget local newspapers. You may never have read the 'Townville Bugle' before, but it may contain salvation now.

8. Respond to advertisements

Begin to prepare a CV or update the one which you already have. As an alternative, prepare a biographical note which may allow you to be more selective and flexible. However, remember that a biographical note is not a licence to mislead potential employers. Remember:

- covering letters should be brief and give clear, positive reasons for considering your CV
- CVs should not exceed two sides of A4 in length
- your CV is competing with others for the reader's time
- the best CVs contain positive statements rather than a mere chronology of dates and titles

- professional presentation using white space makes a document more attractive and readable.

Check with a friend – does your proposed CV show you to the best advantage and is it free from spelling mistakes/grammatical errors?

There are professional CV writers who advertise in the national press – but ask for a sample of their work before you commission them. You may be spending money for a mass-produced 'product' which does not reflect your individuality or achievement.

9. Beware

- Don't rush prematurely into a 'job wanted' advertisement. They are expensive and the success rate is said to be very low.
- Be careful of firms which advertise 'access to the unadvertised job market'. Some are professional and ethical; some only wish to sell you a 'complete', very expensive package. They offer CV preparation, counselling, often of dubious quality, and a training course in self-presentation. Ask for introductions to people whom they have helped find a real job.
- Don't send your CV to every head-hunter and recruitment consultant you can identify through newspapers and periodicals. You will spend a lot of money for almost certainly no return. They work for organisations, not for individuals.

10. Find out about your rights

By now you may be thinking about your rights as a redundant person. Before rushing off to see a solicitor, consider:

- the Job Centre
- the Citizens Advice Bureau
- the Careers Advisory Service
- your professional body.

They may all be able to help or reassure you, without your incurring the expense of a lawyer. At the same time, find out if there are 'job clubs' in your area. These are places where similarly unemployed professionals meet, to work together towards finding jobs and to reassure each other that redundant people are human beings with talents and competences to offer.

11. Take stock of your finances

Your 'rights' will have included a financial settlement, if only at the statutory minimum level. Take complete stock of your assets and liabilities. Don't overvalue your capital items. Consider how you can cut your costs but don't rush into dramatic decisions until you are in a stable frame of mind to make them. Don't say 'We are going to maintain our standard of living whatever happens'. You may be unemployed for longer than you think. Think in terms of 'investing' rather than spending. Ask whether each item of expenditure is an investment towards obtaining a new job. Ask before you invest and not after the money has been spent.

12. Record and plan

Record the day's achievements and make a plan for tomorrow. You may feel that it is time to start calling your list of potential helpers on the telephone but be sure that you are in the right mood before you do so. Rehearse, aloud, what you are going to say and how you will say it. Remember that once an unfortunate impression has been made on the telephone, it is impossible to recall it.

13. Keep fit and healthy

If you have been too busy for exercise and fresh air perhaps you can end the day by taking a brisk stroll. Remember that your new job is finding a new job and you will be able to do it more effectively if you are fit and well.

Dos and don'ts for the next day

Do
- Consider all your options – they may extend beyond looking for the same kind of job.
- Recognise that 'it' has happened to many other people and try to remember that you have not been singled out for a unique fate.
- Consider the possibility of temporary part-time work for a voluntary organisation; this helps you to feel valued and provides a routine – and it may also give you your next contacts.

Don't
- Waste your nervous energy and the goodwill of your friends by telling them over and over again that you have been unfairly treated.
- Devote precious time to asking yourself 'why me?'
- Delay – face up to the situation and 'get on with it'.

Useful reading

BOOKS

Breakthrough: handling career opportunities and changes, Anthony Weldon, London: Bene Factum, 1993

Guidance through redundancy, Corby: Institute of Management, 1993

How to survive redundancy: a practical guide to help you cope, Judy Skeats, Peterborough: Pearl Assurance

JOURNAL ARTICLES

Escape from the black hole, David Goodhart, Financial Times, 29 Aug 1992, pp6

Facing redundancy: be positive, Management Week, Aug no 7 1991, pp58–59

Thought starters

- Redundancy – a blow but also an opportunity?
- Whom have you helped in the past?
- What advice would you give to someone in the same position?
- You've got a lot to offer – have you always packaged it to the best advantage?
- It may be hard but people prefer smilers to moaners.

Choosing a Second Career

This checklist offers a framework within which the objectives and choices open to you in choosing a second career can be identified. It is addressed to those who see themselves presented with an opportunity to choose a second career and to those who, for a variety of reasons, feel that pursuit of an earlier career is either impossible or undesirable.

MCI Standards

This checklist has relevance for the MCI Management Standards: Key Role C – Manage People.

Definition

A career is the job or profession that someone does for a period of their life, not necessarily with the same employer. Planning for a second career implies embarking on a course of action which will lead to the pursuit of a different job, profession or occupation for a significant number of years.

For some, the need – or opportunity – to choose a second career has always existed. Members of the armed forces, and of the police and fire services, for example, have always retired earlier than much of the population. Today, developments in the world of work – growth in the number of mergers taking place, downsizing, outsourcing and early retirement policies – have left more of us confronted with choices about how we spend the last ten or more years of our working lives.

Advantages of choosing a second career

- New interests and a new lease of life.
- New friends, colleagues and associates.
- Opportunities to test yourself against new challenges.

Disadvantages of choosing a second career

- These depend on your temperament – do you have the energy, enthusiasm and commitment to 'start again', especially in your middle years?

Action checklist

1. Decide whether you are faced with a problem or an opportunity

Be clear about the circumstances in which you are even considering a second career. Decide whether you have a problem caused, for example, by redundancy or collapse of your existing business, or a short-term problem caused by personal conflict at work. Consider whether you have an opportunity which is the result of earlier than normal retirement (armed services, police or fire service) together with a pension which will provide you with a basic standard of living whatever the outcome of embarking on a second career. Recognise that a problem needs a solution but that perception of that solution as a second career may be wishful thinking. Recognise also that an opportunity needs a decision and that a decision requires assessment of information and facts.

2. Decide whether you need a second career or just another employer

You may feel disillusioned with your profession and with the market sector in which you work. Be clear, however, that this is not a good reason for seeking to change your career unless you are satisfied that you have some talent in other areas of activity. Ask yourself whether you are being realistic in attempting a drastic change. Consider whether your interests have changed, or whether your balance of skills has shifted, or whether you feel you need a new stimulus. Talk to colleagues and friends. Satisfy yourself that you really do want a career change rather than just a new job.

3. Decide on your objectives, motives and priorities

Decide whether your aim is to:

- enhance your income, be it from pension, investments or other sources
- provide yourself with an income which will provide you and your family with a living
- develop a completely new career with skills which you have not used before either with an employer or in a self-employed capacity
- contribute your skills and experience to the benefit of others.

4. Consider the financial issues involved in choosing a second career

Calculate how much capital you have available for investment in a new career. Be realistic – you may decide to sell your house, but how quickly and at what price? Think about where you will live as an alternative. Be clear in your own mind about the consequences of a relocation.

Calculate how much you need to live on and consider carefully how much you are prepared to spend, invest or lose.

Consider the implications for your family's welfare, your children's education or other aspects of life which are personal and specific to your situation.

5. Think about training

Discover what training you will need for this second career. Find out how it can be obtained, who are the providers, how long it will take, how it may be funded and where it will take place. If it is in a location away from your present home, consider whether you are prepared to be away from your family for a significant period and if they will support you in this. Remember that to move your family to the place where the training will take place will take time, money and nervous energy. Reflect that soon after you have moved, a second move may be necessary to enable you to pursue your second career. Consider the implications for family life, education and a partner's job or career. Remember too that some skills can be self-developed, without 'training'.

6. Consider status

Reflect on your previous status and the power and influence you may have held. Ask yourself how willingly you would forgo these. Ask yourself if you would be prepared to start again at the bottom – or even the middle – of the hierarchy. Remember that you can discuss this question with whom you choose – or with no-one but yourself. You do not have to tell anyone that you couldn't bear a loss of status and prestige but you must be prepared to recognise the fact.

7. Establish what you are good at

Consider what you think you are good at and reflect on your career so far. Does it show that, for example, you are good at problem solving, at your best in situations involving other people's problems, or outstanding in crises? Compare what you are good at with what you may want to do. Consider vocational guidance but remember that it may cost money. Consult a Careers Advisory Service or Counsellor and find out if your local library, Training and Enterprise Council or Business Link can help. Again, ask close friends what they think you are good at – it is easy to over- or underestimate abilities.

8. Discover the demand for what you want to do

Be sure that there is a demand for what you want to do and that the demand exists in places to which you would – and could – happily relocate. Contact your local Job Centre to establish local levels of demand for particular skills, for example. At the same time, remember that you may not possess those skills yet.

9. Consider voluntary work

Voluntary work can provide great satisfaction. REACH is one example of an organisation which needs volunteers to help with social problems and to help the less well-off in a range of charitable activities. BESO seeks those able to offer help, in developing countries, by passing on their skills, by providing organisational support and by direct action in leading projects. Your local Council for Voluntary Organisations may be able to put you in touch with an organisation looking for particular skills.

10. Talk to other people

Talk to others who have taken the path that you are now considering. Try to find those who decided against seeking a second career and discover why they reached that decision. Talk to those who tried but did not succeed – what were the obstacles which they could not overcome? Recognise that they may not have failed because their choice of second career was bad but perhaps because of their own lack of the talent required.

Dos and don'ts for choosing a second career

Do

- Research every aspect of a second career before you abandon your original choice.
- Talk to people who have embarked on the second career which you favour and ask about the downside as well as the good points.
- Hesitate before you invest precious capital without solid evidence that you are not throwing your money away.

Don't

- Abandon everything because you know you are following a 'sure bet'.
- Be carried away by the glamour of what you have in mind.
- Do you need to make a living? Does this job, profession or occupation offer you more than a reasonable chance of doing so?

Useful reading

BOOKS

Assessing your career: time for a change, Ben Ball, Leicester: BPS Books, 1996

Change: an opportunity in disguise, Gordon Crawford, Crows Nest, Australia: Little Hills Press, 1992

Parting company: how to survive the loss of a job and find another successfully, Rev ed, William J Morin and James C Cabrera, San Diego, Calif: Harvest Harcourt Brace Jovanovich, 1991

The mid career action guide: a practical guide to mid career change, Derek Kemp and Fred Kemp, London: Kogan Page, 1991

Changing course: how to take charge of your career, Sue Dyson and Stephen Hoare, London: Sheldon Press, 1990

The inventurers: excursions in life and career renewal, 3rd ed, Janet Hagberg and Richard Leider Reading, MA: Addison Wesley, 1988

Thought starters

- Steam engines were fun, but they're obsolete!
- Where and what do I want to be in ten years' time?
- What am I good at as opposed to what would I like to be good at?
- Many of the very large percentage of small businesses which fail each year are started by those who believe, romantically, that a second career offered a better option than continuation of the career which had served them well until a major problem arose.

Planning your Retirement

This checklist is designed to help managers planning for their own retirement. Good planning needs to start early in order to enjoy many years of active and fruitful life beyond the retirement date. Taking personal responsibility for your retirement is becoming increasingly essential.

MCI Standards

This checklist has relevance for the MCI Management Standards: Key Role C – Manage People.

Definition

Retirement may mean the end of paid full-time employment, but with increased longevity and better health many more people can now look forward to 20 years or more in retirement. This is a large slice of life which needs to be planned for so that it may be both comfortable and enjoyable. Planning, particularly financial planning, needs to be long-term.

Advantages of planning your retirement

Planning your retirement can:

- remove anxiety about your money, about what you can do and whether you can cope
- enable you to look forward with confidence to a new phase of your life
- enable you to develop yourself in ways you have not had the opportunity to do before.

Disadvantages of failing to plan your retirement

Failure to plan for retirement may result in:

- anxiety about your finances
- anxiety about a loss of identity when you give up work
- missing a secure daily routine and finding it hard to change
- worrying about what you will do with your spare time
- missing the personal contacts work has provided.

Action checklist

1. Adopt a positive attitude

Growing older happens to everyone and is something to be accepted. It allows a fresh start to a new way of life, and so is to be welcomed rather than feared. However it helps to be aware beforehand and to make sensible plans.

2. Plan your finances

One of the commonest fears about retirement is whether there will be enough money to enjoy it. You will want to aim to maintain the standard of living in retirement that you have had during your working life. Take advantage of any pre-retirement counselling or courses offered.

You need to know your likely retirement income. Find out:

- how much your company pension will be. You should receive regular statements on this. If you have changed employers you should make sure you also have statements on any earlier entitlements you may have. It is likely that you may have the option of taking part of the pension as a lump sum. This is generally regarded as a valuable option, particularly if you have a partner. But if your scheme provides total or substantial inflation protection you should think hard about sacrificing it for a lump sum. You need also to look at your health and your family record of longevity though you are statistically likely to live 3–5 years longer than your parents. If you are reinvesting the sum, will the yield from the investment and the protection of your capital be as good as the pension given up?

- how much your state retirement pension is likely to be, including, if applicable, additional pension (SERPS) and graduated pension.

- what your Additional Voluntary Contributions (AVCs) are likely to amount to and how this sum may be invested. Ideally you should start, or have started, to contribute to these in your mid- or late forties. Generally AVCs have to be used to purchase an annuity. Most schemes will offer you an annuity scheme, but if you are single, for example, this may not be the most advantageous available. Shop around.

If you start your planning early, say 10 years before retirement, you may be able to improve your position, and you should make sure you are aware of what is possible with AVCs.

If you have a partner then look at the position jointly. It is important to keep up-to-date with changes, particularly in taxation. It may, for example, be advantageous for the partner with the lower income to hold a larger slice of the investments. Your financial planning must take taxation into account and you should ensure you have at least an elementary knowledge of allowances, the tax bands and the position of your partner.

Unless you are an expert it is helpful to have a financial adviser. The authority to offer financial advice is strictly controlled. To cover all your needs it is probably best to seek an independent financial adviser who is not tied to the products of a particular investment house.

3. Make a Will

If you have already made a Will, then retirement is a good time to check it and make sure it is still appropriate. If you have not already made a Will, retirement is a good time to do so. When you make a Will you are thinking of others, not just who gets what but saving in worry and anguish; dying intestate can make things difficult for your heirs. You can obtain a form with simple instructions from a stationers, but there are pitfalls and it is better to get a Solicitor to draw it up for you. If you want to pass on substantial sums to your children, it may be best to pass some over earlier to avoid death duties. Having made your Will, make sure your executors and partner (or close relatives) know where it is kept.

4. Cater for the even older generation

With improved health and diet people live longer and at retirement you may find yourself with responsibility for, or the need to help, your parents or elderly relatives. They may need you to help move them into some form of sheltered housing, help in managing their affairs or help them obtain benefits to which they are entitled. Again forethought and planning can make a difference. Some useful addresses are given at the end of this checklist.

5. Plan where you are going to live

You may dream of retiring to some beloved holiday spot, returning to the place where you grew up, moving nearer your children or looking for somewhere warm and retiring abroad. For some, these ideas may work out, but for many they may be a disaster. Go to the chosen place and see it at its worst; think about whom you will know there. While it could be lovely to start with, think how it will be as you get older.

It may be better to stay put and in that case take a critical look at your home. Is it too big? People often think something smaller would be good for retirement but you will be there all the time. Is there room for your planned leisure activities? Do you need some kind of home office? Is it easy to run and to heat? Think about improvements or changes, safety (how old is your wiring?), managing your garden in 10 or 20 years' time (can you make it easier?), and transport (what will you need?).

6. Plan for your leisure and health

You have spent around 2,000 hours a year at work and this may at first seem a daunting time to fill. You may want to think about some part-time work at least to start with, particularly if you are retiring early. There is an increasing demand for the skills of older people on a short-term or part-time basis. The most essential ingredient is to be flexible in your approach.

Short-term or part-time earnings will affect your tax position and you should check this when accepting a job or assignment. They will not, how-ever, affect your entitlement to your organisation or state pension.

There is unlimited scope for those who wish to give their time to voluntary work. Most towns have a volunteer bureau or a Council for Voluntary Service which know of local needs. Check in your local telephone directory. Many national organisations would like help at local level and your manage-ment skills are likely to be welcomed.

You probably have some hobby or pastime you have been planning to develop in retirement. If you have not, try to cultivate one, particularly one involving physical exercise. Walking or cycling are two obvious ones and both can be linked well with other hobbies such as photography, sketching or bird-watching. If you are already a golfer you will be looking forward to playing more mid-week.

If you want to exercise your brain there are many opportunities for learning both through correspondence and residential courses. Many counties have residential training centres offering a wide variety of courses; get hold of a copy of their brochures.

Make sure you have plenty of social contacts. Even if you have a partner, each of you should have your own social life if you are not to be in danger of boring one another. Have a health check on or before retirement. At best, this will reassure you; at worst, it will guide you as to what you should and shouldn't do.

For a healthy, happy retirement a balance of activities seems to be best, but a reasonable amount of physical exercise is important. Pay attention to your diet.

7. Plan holidays

Holidays are just as important in retirement as before. But now you can take them as you wish and have the advantage of off-peak prices, mid-week travel, short-notice departure, off-season discounts and longer-stay holidays. Check your home insurance to make sure you are covered if you are away more than 30 days. Get a neighbour to keep an eye on your property and if it is in winter make sure you take precautions against burst pipes and the like. It may be worthwhile getting hold of brochures from specialist operators such as Saga to see the range of holidays on offer. Some organisations also offer arrangements for long distance flights at advantageous rates without taking a full package.

If you are likely to take a number of holidays each year, consider taking out an annual travel insurance policy rather than paying a premium for each holiday.

8. Adjust

Remember that in retirement you are a new boy/girl. You are doing it for the first time. You should discuss the 'chores' with your partner and work out fair shares. It is a good idea to do more things together but also to have some activities you each do on your own. All cooking and housework should not remain purely feminine activities, if they ever were. Similarly business matters, tax returns and finances should not be male preserves, but should be shared and understood by both partners. Don't take over too many household duties, or your partner may feel deprived and unneeded.

Retirement is an opportunity not a calamity! Enjoy it!

Dos and don'ts for retirement

Do

- Plan your finances.
- Find something worthwhile to do.
- Consider your partner.
- Always have something to look forward to.

Don't

- Rush into unwise decisions about finance or where to live.

Useful reading

BOOKS

Good non-retirement guide, Rosemary Brown, London: Kogan Page, 1995

The Penguin financial guide to a successful retirement, Alison Mitchell and Wendy Elkington, London: Penguin Books, 1993

Making the most of your retirement: a practical guide, 2nd ed, Keith Hughes, London: Kogan Page, 1989

JOURNAL ARTICLE

Pre-retirement factsheet, Rosemary Brown, Personnel Management, Nov vol 22 no 11 1990, Factsheet 35

Useful addresses

Age Concern England, 1268 London Road, London SW16 4ER, Tel: 0181 679 8000

Ashton Penney Partnership Ltd, Head Office, Suite 201, Albany House, 324–326 Regent Street, London Wl4 5AA, Tel: 0171 580 8490 Fax: 0171 580 8376

Business in the Community, 227a City Road, London, EClV lLX, Tel: 0171 253 3716

IMRO (Investment Management Regulatory Organisation), Broadwalk House, Appold Street, London EC2A 2LL, Tel: 0171 628 6022

PIA (Personal Investment Authority), 1 Canada Square, Canary Wharf, London E14 5AZ, Tel: 0171 538 8860

Saga Leisure Ltd, The Saga Building, Middleburg Square, Folkstone, Kent, CT20 1AZ, Tel: 01303 711111 Fax: 01303 256676

Thought starters

- Have you made a retirement budget?
- Have you set up a retirement planner for retirement activities?

Further *Business Checklists* titles from Hodder & Stoughton and the Institute of Management all at £8.99

0 340 74292 5	Information & Financial Management	❏
0 340 74290 9	Marketing & Strategy	❏
0 340 74291 7	Operations & Quality Management	❏
0 340 74288 7	People Management	❏
0 340 74289 5	Personnel Policies, Training & Development	❏
0 340 74293 3	Small Business Management	❏

All Hodder & Stoughton books are available from your local bookshop or can be ordered direct from the publisher. Just tick the titles you want and fill in the form below. Prices and availability subject to change without notice.

To: Hodder & Stoughton Ltd, Cash Sales Department, Bookpoint, 78 Milton Park, Abingdon, Oxon OX14 4TD. If you have a credit card you may order by telephone – 01235 400414

fax – 01235 400454

E-mail address: orders@bookpoint.co.uk

Please enclose a cheque or postal order made payable to Bookpoint Ltd to the value of the cover price and allow the following for postage and packaging:

UK & BFPO: £4.30 for one book; £6.30 for two books; £8.30 for three books.

OVERSEAS & EIRE: £4.80 for one book; £7.10 for 2 or 3 books (surface mail).

Name: ....

Address: ....

....

....

If you would prefer to pay by credit card, please complete:

Please debit my Visa/Mastercard/Diner's Card/American Express (delete as appropriate) card no:

❏ ❏ ❏ ❏ ❏ ❏ ❏ ❏ ❏ ❏ ❏ ❏ ❏ ❏ ❏

Signature .... Expiry date ....